F. Scott

FITZGERALD

F. Scott FITZGERALD

THE AMERICAN DREAMER

By

John Tessitore

FRANKLIN WATTS
A Division of Scholastic Inc.
New York • Toronto • London • Auckland • Sydney
Mexico City • New Delhi • Hong Kong
Danbury, Connecticut

Interior design by Sue Carlson

Library of Congress Cataloging-in-Publication Data

Tessitore, John.
  F. Scott Fitzerald : the American dreamer / by John Tessitore.
    p.   cm.
  Includes bibliographical references and index.
  ISBN 0-531-13955-7
    1. Fitzgerald, F. Scott (Francis Scott), 1896–1940—Juvenile liter-
  ature. 2. Authors, American—20th century—Biography—Juvenile
  literature. [1. Fitzgerald, F. Scott (Francis Scott), 1896–1940. 2.
  Authors, American.] I. Title.

  PS3511.I9 Z873 2001
  813'.52—dc21
  [B]   00-068647

CONTENTS

INTRODUCTION

She was a sun, radiant, growing, gathering light and
storing it—then after an eternity pouring it forth in a
glance, the fragment of a sentence, to that part of him
that cherished all beauty and illusion.
—From *The Beautiful and Damned*[1]

Every New York gossip columnist seemed to tell a different
version of the story.

Everyone agreed that F. Scott Fitzgerald and his wife
Zelda had danced in the city's public fountains, but they disagreed about the details. Some said Zelda began the trend by
diving fully clothed into the fountain at Union Square. Others
said she frolicked naked in the fountain at Washington Square.
Still others said that Scott refused to be outdone, and skipped
into the Pulitzer Fountain outside the Plaza Hotel. Perhaps
they jumped in together, some finally suggested.[2]

The fountain-dancing story took on a life of its own when
it appeared in newspaper society pages in 1920. It quickly
became a part of Manhattan's legend. Perhaps it would have
been ignored, or ridiculed, if it were not about F. Scott Fitzgerald and his wife. Certainly it centered on an insignificant event
in the life of a big city. In the twenties, New York was full of
people doing outlandish things. But the Fitzgeralds were different. They were beautiful and young and bold and very, very
talented. Scott had just published his first novel, *This Side of
Paradise*, and had become an overnight sensation. An entire

Zelda and Scott Fitzgerald were considered the "it" couple
of the Jazz Age.

generation of Americans now looked to the Fitzgeralds as
models of a new, modern lifestyle. Scott and Zelda ushered in
an era of cultural freedom, economic prosperity, and good-
natured excess, an era when people danced in public fountains
to celebrate the sheer joy of living. Scott would even give the
era its name: the Jazz Age.

Like all historical periods, the Jazz Age would come to an

end. And Scott and Zelda would lose their standing as the most glamorous couple in America. In fact, their moment in the spotlight, like the Jazz Age itself, would end tragically.

Future generations would regard F. Scott Fitzgerald as one of the greatest writers in American literary history, and his 1925 novel, *The Great Gatsby*, as one of the best works of fiction ever written. But Scott experienced more than his share of failure during his lifetime. That is why, late in life, he looked back on his early days in New York and mourned his happy youth. He remembered being a different person—wide eyed, carefree, and brave enough to dance in public fountains:

> And there are still times when I creep up on him, surprise him on an autumn morning in New York or a spring night in Carolina when it is so quiet that you can hear a dog barking in the next country. But never again as during that all too short period when he and I were one person, when the fulfilled future and the wistful past were mingled in a single gorgeous moment—when life was literally a dream.[3]

Chapter 1

ST. PAUL

He was planning his life. He was going to live in New York, and be known at every restaurant and café, wearing a dress-suit from early evening to early morning, sleeping away the dull hours of the forenoon.
—From *This Side of Paradise*[1]

In 1896, St. Paul, Minnesota, was a half century old, a relatively new city on the American landscape. Originally a station for steamboats that traveled along the Mississippi River, it became a major railroad hub in the mid-1860s and the eastern terminus of the Great Northern Railroad in 1879, when the city's most influential resident, James J. Hill, consolidated several smaller train lines into a single service that crossed the Northwest to Seattle. Hill's railroad improved transcontinental shipping and travel and ushered in a period of great prosperity for St. Paul's residents.

For Francis Scott Key Fitzgerald, who was born in St. Paul on September 24, 1896, the city was a symbol of individual ambition and achievement. To Scott (as he was called by friends and family), St. Paul was a tangible product of the American Dream, in which men like James J. Hill, combining great wealth with personal power, could literally create a new world. All his life, Scott would seek out traces of this world-creating power in himself. Above all, he wanted to be important the way Hill was important. His search for influence, for greatness, would inspire his major works of fiction, the novels and stories that redefined the American character. And for brief and scattered moments, he even seemed to achieve a measure of greatness himself.

Scott's father, Edward Fitzgerald, was born on Glenmary Farm near Rockville, Maryland, in 1853. Edward descended from one of the first Catholic families to settle the Maryland colony in the seventeenth century. Among his famous ancestors were Philip Barton Key, an early congressman and Supreme Court lawyer, and Scott's namesake, Francis Scott Key, the Baltimore lawyer who wrote "The Star Spangled Banner" during the War of 1812. Edward, his brother John, and his sister Eliza represented the fifth generation of Fitzgeralds to live on Glenmary Farm.[2] The family took pride in its Southern heritage and values and sympathized with the Confederacy during the Civil War. Young Edward even assisted Confederate spies who worked along the Potomac River, outside Washington, D.C. After the Union victory in 1865, the Fitzgeralds tried to preserve some of the more praiseworthy aspects of Southern culture. Throughout his life, Edward would maintain high standards for personal honor, gentlemanly conduct, and upright appearances (including a fondness for well-tailored clothes and shined shoes). But he would never learn to thrive in the harsh, impersonal world of the postwar business environment.

In 1890, having dropped out of Georgetown University and failing to make his fortune in Chicago, Edward moved to the booming city of St. Paul. There he met Mary "Mollie" McQuillan, the oldest daughter of Philip Francis McQuillan, a man with one of the most unusual success stories of his era. Philip McQuillan's parents fled Ireland in 1842, three years before the famine that sent thousands of impoverished Irish families to America's shores. They settled in Galena, Illinois. At twenty-three, Philip left Galena to become a bookkeeper for the St. Paul wholesale grocer Baupré & Temple. After an extraordinary rise through the company ranks, Philip took over Baupré & Temple in 1872 and, by 1875, it occupied the largest building in town, a five-story giant. He moved his family into a mansion on Summit Avenue, the most exclusive neighborhood in St. Paul, close to the home of his friend, railroad financier James J. Hill. When Philip died in 1877 of lung problems and a liver disorder called Bright's Disease, he left his family a fortune estimated at $400,000. His wife Louisa sold the mansion, but she purchased a new house close by in order to maintain her position within St. Paul's elite society. She and her children continued to practice their Catholic faith devoutly and live comfortable lives long after Philip's death.

In 1890, Edward Fitzgerald married Mollie McQuillan, whom one relative called "the most awkward and the homeliest woman I ever saw."[3] Born in 1860, Mollie received her education first at a St. Paul convent and then at New York's Manhattanville College, where she acquired a love of books but a rather peculiar taste for melodramatic literature. In some ways, her literary tastes mirrored her strange personal habits: She seemed to accentuate her strong, harsh features by dressing outlandishly, carrying an umbrella in fine weather, and wearing mismatched shoes. Perhaps unintentionally, she cultivated a reputation for tactlessness, often making offensive remarks without concern for the effects they had on people. She was, in short, the perfect opposite of her meek but courtly husband, a fact that became clear during their honeymoon visit to Paris. Edward, who appreciated high culture but did not have the financial means to live lavishly, urged her to dress quickly for a tour of the city. Mollie, who was used to a comfortable lifestyle and had visited Europe before, insensitively replied, "But I've already seen Paris!"[4] Thus began the odd union between Mollie, with her expectations for comfort and luxury, and Edward, who would never measure up the McQuillan family legacy.

Their impressionable son Scott would adopt his parents' best and worst traits. He would emulate his father's sense of style but regret his father's weaknesses; he would admire the McQuillans' drive for success but deplore his mother's selfishness and erratic behavior. And although he would always try to negotiate a third way to live, he would repeat his parents'

Scott's eccentric mother, Mollie Fitzgerald,
in a 1905 photograph

mistakes: He'd be stylish and weak like Edward, driven and erratic like Molly.

In 1896, the year of Scott's birth, an epidemic swept through St. Paul. Both the Fitzgeralds' older daughters—three-year-old Louise and one-year-old Mary—died. Another Fitzgerald infant died an hour after birth in 1900, leaving Scott an only child until his sister Annabel was born in 1901. Blond and blue-eyed, susceptible to bronchitis, Scott became the sole object of his mother's affections and a coddled, spoiled child. When Scott was born, Edward owned the American Rattan and Willow Works, a St. Paul furniture manufacturer, and the family enjoyed a measure of prominence and independence from the McQuillan family fortune. But the business collapsed in 1898, forcing the Fitzgeralds out of St. Paul. Edward found work as a soap salesman for Procter & Gamble, canvassing the cities of Buffalo and, later, Syracuse in upstate New York. These moves, in addition to the summers Scott spent with relatives in Maryland—Mollie believed the Southern climate would improve his health—forced Scott to re-create friendships on a frequent basis. A stubborn, egotistical child, he seldom succeeded in making himself popular. For the most part, he grew up a social outcast and a self-absorbed dreamer. One year, his mother tried to improve his standing by throwing him a birthday party, but no one attended. She sent him to summer camp in Canada, but he forged no lasting bonds.[5] Nevertheless, Scott was determined to achieve a popularity reserved for more athletic, more personable, and wealthier children. As he searched for social acceptance, he developed an intense shame for his odd mother as well as his family's financial difficulties. "[T]hough I would like very much to have you up here I don't think you would like it," he told Mollie in a letter from summer camp politely asking her not to embarrass him by visiting. "Please send me a dollar because there are a lot of little odds and ends I need. I will spend it causiusly. All the other boys have pocket money besides their regular allowence."[6]

Both the concerns Scott expressed in this letter—his embarrassment about his family's eccentricities and his desire for financial security—culminated in 1908, when Edward lost

Edward Fitzgerald with his son Scott, Christmas 1899

his job with Procter & Gamble. This catastrophe sent Edward and Mollie Fitzgerald back to St. Paul, where they would subsist on Mollie's inheritance for the rest of their lives. For almost a year, Scott and Annabel lived on Laurel Avenue with Louisa McQuillan while their parents lived with friends on Summit Avenue. Edward set up a wholesale grocery brokerage from his brother-in-law's real estate office, but would never be able to support his family again. In desperation, he turned to liquor and, in time, became a mild-mannered, ineffectual alcoholic. Despite their geographic proximity to Summit Avenue, the Fitzgeralds retreated from the high society that had once welcomed them. The tragedy of their situation did not escape the notice of the young, socially insecure Scott.

To make matters worse, Scott attended St. Paul Academy in the fall of 1908, where he studied alongside the sons of the local elite. Still desperate to make friends, and now uncertain of his social status, he tried too hard to impress his peers. He wanted them to admire him for his athletic ability, but he was too small and timid to succeed on the football field or basketball court—though, surprisingly, he was elected captain of the basketball team in 1911. Instead, he convinced them of his intellectual superiority, an easier task given his passion for reading and his ability to fake a familiarity with books he had not read. But even Scott knew that scholarship alone would not gain for him the popularity he sought. And his classmates soon tired of his endless campaigning; one boy even wrote an article in the school magazine asking for someone to "poison Scotty or find some means to shut his mouth."[7] The only thing that brought him any real success or happiness during his three years at St. Paul Academy was his work for the school's drama club and newspaper. Lazy in most other aspects of his life, Scott worked hard at his writing. "When it came to rewriting," remembered the drama club's director, Elizabeth Magoffin, "Fitzgerald was indefatigable, retiring to a corner and tossing off new lines with his ever-facile pen."[8] In 1909, the school's magazine, *Now and Then*, published his story "The Mystery of the Raymond Mortgage," a mystery modeled after the haunting tales of Edgar Allan Poe. It was the first of several stories

Scott at age fifteen

and articles Scott would publish in the years to come. As he developed his fiction-writing skills, he also nurtured a lifelong interest in the theater, visiting the local vaudeville theater every Saturday and writing his own plays, four of which would be produced by the St. Paul theater group over the next four summers. During the 1914 performance of his play *Assorted Spirits,* he even exhibited a flair for the kind of unpredictable show-manship that would make him famous, and ultimately infamous, later in life. When an electrical fuse exploded in the theater and frightened the audience, he leapt onto the stage and delivered an improvised monologue to calm the crowd. Within the con-text of his writing—for the stage or for print—the delicately handsome Scott appeared to be in complete control.

Unfortunately, he paid far less attention to his academic assignments and grades. Aside from his extracurricular writing, Scott performed poorly during all three years at St. Paul. As a result, during the summer of 1911, his parents decided that he needed a stricter program and a more demanding environ-ment. They settled on The Newman School in Hackensack, New Jersey, an exclusive academy for the sons of the nation's most influential Catholic families. At Newman, his old charac-ter flaws resurfaced. His roommate remembered that he had "the most impenetrable egotism" he had ever seen.[9] Too selfish and vain to make friends naturally, and too small and weak to impress anyone physically, Scott relied on his pen (and St. Paul Academy's summertime productions of his plays) for acclaim and social stature. His first two semesters were particularly dif-ficult, though he improved his grades enough to earn an occa-sional pass to Manhattan, 10 miles (16 kilometers) from Hackensack, where he attended the Broadway musicals he soon learned to imitate.

Despite the hardships of his first year away from home, Scott finished on a positive note, surpassing even his own expectations by winning several events at a spring track-and-field meet. Riding a wave of success, he then broke into the mainstream culture at Newman to begin his second year. He befriended Charles "Sap" Donahoe, a brilliant student and star football player whose favorable opinion helped make Scott a more popular figure at the school. He continued to excel at track and field and improved his skills on the football field. He published stories in the *Newman News*. And, most important of all, he attracted the attention of an influential trustee of the school, Father Cyril Sigourney Webster Fay.

Thirty-seven-year-old Father Fay had been ordained a

Catholic priest two years before he met Scott. Before then, he had been an Episcopal minister and a professor of theology at the Nashotah House in Fond du Lac, Wisconsin. But Fay, like Scott, was a spiritual wanderer. After spending years denying the legitimacy of the Roman Catholic Church, he converted in 1910 and accepted a teaching position at Catholic University in Washington, D.C. Always curious and receptive to new ideas, however, he divided his time between his Church duties and a variety of less spiritual pursuits. In fact, he enjoyed a more cosmopolitan lifestyle than many other priests of the age. Grossly overweight but always impeccably dressed, he stressed the development of personal style and charm in himself and in others. He cultivated friendships with the nation's most important artists and scholars. In Scott, he must have recognized a kindred spirit, a boy who seemed equally interested in matters of

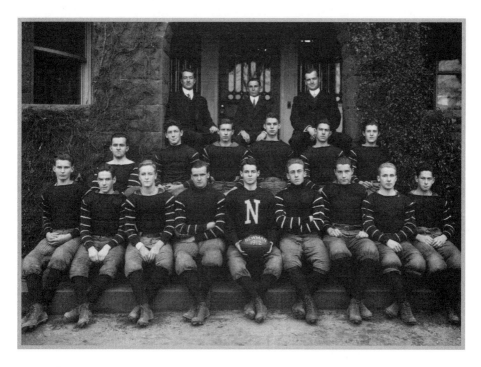

Scott (seated third from the left in the front row) poses with the Newman School football team, 1912.

taste and distinction. He soon became Scott's most important mentor, a father figure to replace the well-meaning but weak Edward Fitzgerald. Fay introduced Scott to new kinds of literature, such as the witty plays of Oscar Wilde, and new kinds of people, such as historian Henry Adams—whose memoir, *The Education of Henry Adams*, would influence Scott's early fiction—and Shane Leslie, a well-connected, well-traveled son of a British nobleman who would assist Scott during the early years of his writing career. Most of all, Fay flattered Scott into believing that he was a special boy, destined for greatness. As a result, he reinforced Scott's weaknesses as well as his strengths. He helped Scott develop his writing talent, but also fed Scott's already troublesome vanity. Under Fay's guidance, Scott blossomed as a writer but withered in ways that would become more obvious during his occasionally glorious but often troubled days at Princeton.

Chapter 2

SPIRES AND GARGOYLES

> The night mist fell. From the moon it rolled, clustered
> about the spires and towers, and then settled below
> them, so that the dreaming peaks were still in lofty aspi-
> ration toward the sky.
>
> —From *This Side of Paradise*[1]

Scott's grandmother, Louisa McQuillan, died in the summer of 1913. In her will, she left Mollie's family $125,000. Scott, who had been contemplating a college career at Georgetown or the University of Minnesota, now set his sights on the more prestigious Princeton. He had considered other Ivy League universities as well; he found Harvard too dull and Yale too crass. But Princeton, as he wrote in his first novel, *This Side of Paradise*, had an "atmosphere of bright colors" and an "alluring reputation as the pleasantest country club in the world."[2] Princeton was the place where he could cultivate his gentlemanly manners as well as the personal connections he would need in order to succeed in the larger world. And it was the home of a heroic, often ill-fated football team. Later in life, Scott would credit a 1911 victory over Harvard as the start of his love affair with Princeton. Finally, and perhaps most importantly, it was the home of the Triangle Club, a theatrical group that produced an acclaimed musical review each year. Weaned on vaudeville and Broadway shows, Scott dreamed of a future in the theater, and the Triangle Club seemed the fastest route to show-business success.

But Scott did not earn high enough grades at St. Paul Academy and Newman to gain immediate admission to Princeton. Forced to take an entrance exam for which he was ill prepared, he cheated during the written portion and failed anyway.[3] During the oral portion, which he took on his seventeenth birthday, he reasoned that he could not be rejected on such a milestone. Compassionately, his examiners eased their standards and admitted him.

Elated and determined to conquer his new surroundings, he wired home asking his mother for his football equipment. He knew that a success on the gridiron would assure him a place of prestige in the Princeton social order. But Scott, a 138-pound (63-kilogram) freshman who had played only a minor role on his prep-school teams, was cut during the first day of tryouts. After this inauspicious start, Scott sought and soon found other ways to distinguish himself from his classmates.

From the beginning, Princeton seemed an enchanted place to Scott. Founded in 1746 as The College of New Jersey, the university changed its name to Princeton, the name of its surrounding town, in 1896, the year Scott was born. Until the mid-nineteenth century, it was the learning institution preferred by the sons of wealthy Southern plantation owners, and it retained some of its Southern heritage well into the twentieth century. Princeton fostered the same elements of taste and refinement that Edward Fitzgerald cultivated from his own Southern background. The campus had been the site of George Washington's first victory as commander of the patriot forces during the American Revolution, when the college's buildings housed Washington's troops. But by the time Scott arrived, the college had been almost completely renovated. It now boasted a student body of about fifteen hundred, a set of neo-Gothic buildings grand enough to support its important and growing reputation and, under the guidance of its esteemed president, Woodrow Wilson (the future 28th president of the United States), it had developed a more demanding curriculum based on the teaching methods of the great British universities at Oxford and Cambridge.

Wilson hired Professor Christian Gauss to improve the

This photograph shows Scott (on the left) with two friends during his freshman year at Princeton.

school's modern languages department, and Gauss provided invaluable guidance and literary training to his gifted students. But Gauss may have been the only faculty member Scott respected. Generally, Scott learned more from his talented classmates than his professors. Sap Donahoe joined Scott in the short migration from Newman to Princeton. During a 1915 vacation at the Donahoe estate in Montana, Sap introduced

Scott to the masculine pursuits of ranch life. Henry Strater, one of the few philosophical radicals on campus, served as a model of integrity and political involvement. John Peale Bishop, the future poet and novelist, broadened Scott's reading interests and forced him to raise his literary standards. And Edmund "Bunny" Wilson, the erudite son of a Princeton lawyer, assumed his role as Scott's "intellectual conscience" early in their relationship, chastising Scott privately and publicly for his personal faults—including his boastfulness and lack of seriousness—as well as his literary failures.[4]

All of these men, especially Bunny Wilson, would continue to exert important influences on Scott after college, and all would resurface in his fiction. But during Scott's first two years at Princeton, the most important figure on campus was Hobey Baker, the star of the football and hockey teams. Handsome, dignified, and enormously talented, Baker was Scott's ideal Princeton student. (Indeed, he was the nation's ideal college student. To memorialize his skill and character, the National Collegiate Athletic Association named its trophy for the year's best hockey player the Hobey Baker Award.) He embodied the virtues Scott sought to adopt as he re-created himself in the Princeton mold. Under Father Fay's tutelage, and with Baker and Bunny Wilson as models, self-creation became Scott's overriding interest during his college years. The spoiled, insecure child who complained of being "a poor boy in a rich town; a poor boy in a rich boy's school; a poor boy in a rich man's club at Princeton" devised a regimen for improving himself and his stature among his peers.[5] Determined to succeed by hard work if not by natural ability, he created a set of standards for personal conduct which he outlined in his personal diaries and, in one extraordinary letter, passed on to his sister for her own use. "A good smile and one that could be assumed at will, is an absolute necessity," he wrote to Annabel in 1915. "You smile on one side which is *absolutely wrong*. Get before a mirror and practise a smile and get a good one, a radiant smile ought to be in the facial vocabulary of every girl."[6] Running on for pages in a similar manner, the letter suggests that Scott had been practicing his own smile and gestures before mirrors and was pleased

The legendary Hobey Baker, 1914

enough with the results to presume some expertise. He may never be as heroic as Hobey Baker, he seemed to suggest, but he would certainly develop impeccable personal habits.

In that same letter to Annabel, Scott referred to girls he met who either succeeded or failed at the disparate elements of presentation that he described. Among his examples was

Ginevra King, whom Scott praised for mastering the art of the "pathetic, appealing look."[7] Ginevra was sixteen years old when Scott first met her during a 1914 Christmas dance. Her family lived in Lake Forest, Illinois, a wealthy suburb of Chicago, but she attended Westover School with one of Scott's childhood friends, Midge Hersey, and accompanied Midge home to St. Paul for the holidays. As Scott suggested in his letter to Annabel, Ginevra was beautiful, flirtatious, and unusually poised for someone so young. She attracted a variety of suitors. And she added Scott, the handsome Princeton student, to her growing army of admirers. For the next two years, they met frequently in New York and Chicago, St. Paul and Lake Forest, as Scott played the role of the moonstruck lover to Ginevra's haughty socialite. Two years older than she, Scott had already suffered through several bouts of puppy love; Ginevra was not his first girlfriend. But he had never allowed himself to become so infatuated with another person until he met Ginevra. She embodied every quality he admired most: physical beauty, poise, wealth, and style. "Oh, it's hard to write you what I really feel when I think of you so much," he wrote during one intense period of infatuation. "You've gotten to mean to me a *dream* that I can't put on paper any more."[8] To Ginevra, however, Scott was one of many romantic interests, and not an especially interesting candidate for a serious relationship. After 1915, they saw each other less frequently. They relied on their correspondence to prolong their romance, but after Ginevra announced that she had married a naval ensign in 1918, Scott resigned himself to defeat. However, Ginevra did not disappear from his life, even if he saw her only once after 1918. He would call her to mind every time he wrote. In some way, she became the model for every Fitzgerald heroine, for every beautiful woman who inspired his heroes' achievements, toyed with their affections, and broke their hearts.

Desperate for the admiration of his classmates as well as the affections of Ginevra King, Scott polished his image and searched for a territory at Princeton to conquer and make his own. Continuing the pattern he had established at St. Paul Academy, he devoted almost all his time and energy to his

Miss Genevra King was Scott's muse throughout
his literary career.

writing. He ignored most of his class work, except the lectures
and assignments of Gauss and the poet/professor Alfred
Noyes, but ultimately wrote twenty-four pieces for *The Nassau
Literary Magazine*, edited by Bunny Wilson, thirty-six pieces
for the *Tiger*, the school's humor magazine, and the lyrics for
three Triangle Club musicals. In October of his first year, already
failing three classes, he focused his efforts on the theater and

worked at a series of minor jobs for that year's Triangle Club performance. After failing another class in the spring, and having to study through the summer to maintain his place at the university, he returned in 1914 to write the book and lyrics for the year's major production, *Fie! Fie! Fi-Fi!* Scott's play differed from previous Triangle Club performances in its use of ragtime jazz and its introduction of a free-spirited, freethinking, free-speaking female character—perhaps inspired by Ginevra King—known as a "flapper." Both were new developments in American society. Jazz introduced innovative sounds, rhythms, and forms—many with African or Caribbean roots—to the nation, heralding a new freedom of expression in music and dance. And the flapper applied new cultural freedoms to her own lifestyle; she lived for her own pleasure, unconstrained by the old demands American society placed on women as wives and homemakers. Simply by writing about what he experienced in St. Paul, or Lake Forest, or Princeton, or New York, Scott was finding his subject matter and his place in the literary world.

After the success of *Fie! Fie! Fi-Fi!*, Scott's classmates looked to him for his wit and lyrical ability. Bunny Wilson, after laboring over the script for the 1915 Triangle Club production, *The Evil Eye*, swallowed his pride and asked Scott for assistance: "Perhaps you can infuse into it some of the fresh effervescence of youth for which you are so justly celebrated."[9] Though Bunny's request emphasized Scott's youthfulness and implied a criticism of Scott's immaturity—Wilson would always be a little jealous of the ease with which his less-educated, less-worldly, less-serious friend could create literary gems—it also served as proof that Scott had finally made himself an important man on campus.

In February 1915, Scott was elected secretary of the Triangle Club. In March, he was elected into Cottage, one of the "big four" fraternity-like clubs that dominated the social life at Princeton. Founded in 1887 and housed in a lavish building near the campus, it remained a favorite of the school's Southern contingent and, like Scott himself, enjoyed a reputation for accepting only the most stylish, genteel, and leisurely of the school's elite. But, throughout Scott's life, each high, happy moment was balanced by a low, even tragic moment. And these successes in early 1915 led to one of his greatest disappointments. As lyricist and star of *The Evil Eye*, Scott was preparing to lead the Triangle Club on its annual national tour, during which they would play to packed theaters in cities across America. Scott reserved for himself the role of a beautiful showgirl (students of Princeton, an all-male college until 1969, played every role in Triangle Club performances). With his fine features and slim physique, he projected enough glamour and feminine beauty to earn a prominent place in the show's publicity photographs, one of which appeared in *The*

This Triangle Club publicity photo, taken in 1915, depicts Fitzgerald as a chorus girl.

New York Times. But just as Christmas vacation and the national tour approached, the Faculty Committee on Non-Athletic Organizations reviewed his grades, which had improved only slightly during his first three years at Princeton, and declared him academically ineligible to participate. At the same time, he contracted malaria, a common disease in the swamplands of central New Jersey, and returned to St. Paul to recuperate. Wilson and Bishop, who resented that Scott's wit and charm often overshadowed their more intellectual literary offerings, sent him off with a poem, published in *The Nassau Literary Magazine*, that recalled the criticisms published by his classmates at the St. Paul Academy years earlier:

> And I could always be cynically amusing at the expense
> Of those who were cleverer than I
> And from whom I borrowed freely,
> But whose cleverness
> Was not the kind that is effective
> In the February of sophomore year. . .
> No doubt by senior year
> I would have been on every committee in college,
> But I made one slip:
> I flunked out in the middle of junior year.[10]

Perhaps Scott was grateful to leave the scene of his humiliation. He stayed in St. Paul through the spring of 1916. He flaunted his Princeton credentials to his childhood friends but debated whether he would ever return. He even considered embarking on a career writing Broadway theatricals. Years later, he would remember these months as a time of crushing depression: "To me college would never be the same. There were to be no badges of pride, no medals, after all. It seemed one March afternoon that I had lost every single thing I wanted."[11]

Frustrated by illness and academic failure just as he was achieving the social prominence he had sought for so long, Scott returned to Princeton in the fall of 1916 to suffer through another year of unfulfilling class work. He and his roommate John Biggs managed to produce a show for the Triangle Club,

Safety First!, but Scott devoted more of his time than ever before to his fiction and poetry. He added the works of politically charged writers such as H. G. Wells and George Bernard Shaw to his personal literary canon, as well as the poems of Rupert Brooke, a poet who died while serving the British navy during the early battles of World War I. He turned away from musical theater and began to dream of his own place within a more literary tradition, writing to Wilson in the fall of 1917, "Do you realize that Shaw is 61, Wells 51, [G. K.] Chesterton 41, [Shane] Leslie 31 and I 21."[12] Mixing the techniques he learned from these writers with his own obsessive interest in the social world of America's young, fashionable elite, he used his fiction primarily to explore his relationship with Ginevra King. Though immature and unpolished, several of the stories he wrote during this final semester at Princeton would serve as trial runs for his first novel, still almost four years in the offing.

When Scott returned to Princeton to begin his senior year in the fall of 1917, he returned to a campus abuzz with talk of the war raging in Europe. Three years earlier, in 1914, a series of complicated conflicts among European nations had threatened the region's stability and resulted in the assassination of Archduke Franz Ferdinand, heir to the Austro-Hungarian Empire controlling much of Eastern Europe. Europe then divided over the proper response to the assassination, along lines of alliance created by century-old treaties. Germany, seeking wealth and empire, led the Central Powers. France and Great Britain, hoping to limit Germany's expansion, led the Allied forces. While the two sides fought battles all over the world, they were evenly matched on the European continent and bogged down in long, dugout trenches that stretched through France and Belgium. The United States, under Woodrow Wilson, tried to maintain its neutrality through the first three years of the war, but finally entered the fray in April 1917 to break the stalemate in favor of the Allies. America's young college men, swept up in a wave of patriotic furor, displayed their bravery by enlisting to fight.

In June, Scott received a letter from Father Fay asking for his assistance on a mysterious mission to Russia. While the war disrupted the Russian government's ability to suppress religious participation, Father Fay wanted to bring the Russian people back to the Roman Catholic Church. Thrilled to participate in a covert operation, Scott immediately agreed. When the mission was called off, Scott—who had received military officer training at Princeton—passed an officer placement exam and prepared to receive a second lieutenant's commission. He returned to Princeton that fall knowing he would soon embark on a war adventure that would present him with new opportunities for social advancement. After receiving his commission in the fall, he wrote his mother a brutally honest letter describing his intentions for joining the struggle:

> About the army please lets not have either tragedy or Heroics because they are equally distasteful to me. I went into this perfectly cold bloodedly and dont sympathize with the
>
> "Give my son to country" etc
> etc
> etc
> or
> "Hero stuff"
>
> because *I just went* and purely for *social reasons*.[13]

Unlike most of his contemporaries who dreamed of achieving glorious reputations founded on acts of wartime bravery, Scott entered the war for the same reasons he entered Princeton: to become a member of an elite society, to earn respect, and to attain social prominence. Hoping to achieve on the battlefield what he could not achieve in college classrooms and clubs, he left Princeton without graduating in October 1917.

Soon thereafter, he found himself on the training grounds of Fort Leavenworth, Kansas, and discovered that he was ill equipped for military life.

Chapter 3

CHASING PARADISE

> The officer looked at Daisy while she was speaking, in a
> way that every young girl wants to be looked at some
> time, and because it seemed romantic to me I have
> remembered the incident ever since.
>
> —From *The Great Gatsby*[1]

Almost immediately after receiving his army commission letter, Scott ordered custom-tailored uniforms from Brooks
Brothers, the exclusive men's shop. War, to Scott, was a
fashionable event, where he would be seen and make a good
impression. But while he may have cut a striking figure in his
elegant clothes—at one point during his years of service, he
wore leather boots and spurs—he proved to be an inept soldier.
At Fort Leavenworth, he trained under the direction of Captain Dwight D. Eisenhower, the future supreme commander of
U.S. forces in World War II and the 34th president of the
United States, but spent more time outlining his first novel
than mastering military maneuvers and protocol. Somehow, he
survived the initial months of training and advanced to Camp
Zachary Taylor near Louisville, Kentucky, with the 45th
Infantry Regiment. In April 1918, the 45th advanced to Camp
Gordon in Augusta, Georgia. Then, in June, the regiment
combined with another regiment of the Ninth Division and
moved to Camp Sheridan near Montgomery, Alabama. Scott
proved unfit for command in each setting. Once, after hearing
his troops complain about the poor quality of army food, he

Scott saw his participation in World War I as an opportunity
to cut a stylish figure and to travel the world.

forced them to double the length of a march. Then he mistakenly instructed a mortar unit to fire live ammunition at another unit during a training session. He even slept through a reveille and missed his commanding general's inspection. "Nobody took Fitzgerald seriously," one of his army colleagues remembered. "His fellow officers generally conceded that he lacked sound judgment. Much of the time he even appeared to lack any independent judgment at all."[2] Only once did he display any of the heroic qualities the army sought in its officers, saving a number of men when a ferry sank in the Tallapoosa River near Montgomery. Nevertheless, the erratic, immature second lieutenant proved a charming, likable character; he looked and spoke like a leader, even if he acted like a fool. So Brigadier General James Augustine Ryan appointed him aide-de-camp, an administrative role in which Scott's appearance and presentation were more valuable assets than they would have been in the muck and trenches of World War I.

Before leaving Princeton in 1917, Scott passed a new manuscript to the men whom he respected most: Shane Leslie, Father Fay, and Professor Christian Gauss. A synthesis of the themes and scenarios he had been exploring in his short fiction, including the representations of his ill-fated love affair with Ginevra King, the manuscript represented a promising but incomplete attempt at a major literary work. Gauss suggested that he revise it before sending it to publishers. Writing furiously during his weekend breaks from his army duties, he finished a second version of the novel, now called "The Romantic Egotist." With Leslie's help, he submitted the novel to Scribner's, a prominent New York publishing firm, in the early winter of 1918. To Bunny Wilson, he described his work confidently, predicting that its innovations and its unsparingly honest account of life at Princeton would make him a celebrity among young readers. "[I]f Scribner takes it," he wrote, "I know I'll wake some morning and find that the debutantes have made me famous over night. I really believe that no one else could have written so searchingly the story of the youth of our generation."[3] Maxwell Perkins, the young Scribner's editor assigned to Scott's manuscript, agreed with the author's assessment. "No [manuscript] novel has come to us for a long time that seemed to display so much originality," Perkins wrote five months after Scott submitted his work. But Scribner's declined to publish "The Romantic Egotist" without further revision. "It seems to us in short that the story does not culminate in anything as it must to justify the reader's interest as he follows it," Perkins continued, "and that it might be made to do so quite consistently with the characters and with its earlier stages."[4] Perkins did not reject the novel; he requested a third rewrite. And Scott was eager to comply, as soon as he could find the time. But in the fall of 1918, he was distracted from his novel by his military responsibilities and by a beautiful, alluring Montgomery girl named Zelda Sayre.

Zelda was born on July 24, 1900, the youngest daughter of a prominent Southern family. Her father, Anthony Sayre, was the son of a newspaper editor, the nephew of a U.S. senator, and Montgomery's city court judge when Zelda was born. He would soon become a justice on the Alabama State Supreme Court. Zelda's mother, Minnie, was the daughter of Willis B. Machen, who had been a Confederate congressman during the Civil War and, later, a U.S. senator from Kentucky. And Zelda, the Sayres' fifth and last surviving child (one child died in infancy), seemed to have inherited all of the family's intelligence and energy, to which she added her striking good looks. As a result, she became the center of the Sayres' attention. "When I was a little girl," she would remember in later years, "I had great confidence in myself, even to the extent of walking by myself against life as it was then. I did not have a single feeling of inferiority, or shyness, or doubt, and no moral principles."[5] She displayed a quick, active intellect, but preferred ballet lessons and parties to her schoolwork. Growing up in the genteel section of Montgomery called "The Hill," where young girls were taught to be well mannered and rather docile, Zelda's independence caused frequent, legendary disruptions. In one instantly famous incident, she called the local fire department to rescue her from the roof of the Sayre house, onto which she then climbed, simply because she was bored. Though voted The Prettiest and The Most Attractive girl in her high school class, she gathered more admirers than close friends. A local newspaper reported that she had "the straightest nose, the most determined little chin and the bluest eyes in Montgomery." She wore makeup at an earlier age than most Montgomery girls, but she evinced very little interest in fashion, except when her mother dressed her for dances.[6]

Two lines of poetry appeared beneath Zelda's high school yearbook photo: "Why should all life be work, when we all can borrow./ Let's only think of today, and not worry about tomorrow."[7] This epigram perfectly described her attitudes when the U.S. war effort began in 1917. Montgomery, as the site of two army camps—Sheridan and Taylor—boomed under a wartime economy and received droves of young soldiers and workers, most of whom jockeyed for the affections of the local girls. Zelda entertained a growing roster of suitors, including fraternity boys from the nearby colleges and military pilots, who flew stunts over the Sayre house to capture her attention. Her flirtations angered Judge Sayre, who expected more decorum and refinement from his youngest daughter. But Zelda was determined to enjoy herself thoroughly, without restraint.

At a country club dance in July 1918, she met Second Lieutenant F. Scott Fitzgerald. A twenty-two-year-old officer, aspiring writer, and Ivy Leaguer, Scott differed from the young men—Southern and athletic—who usually appealed to Zelda. And she, an eighteen-year-old Southern belle, exhibited the charisma of Ginevra King as well as a careless gaiety that Scott admired and, perhaps, envied. Smitten after their first encounter, Scott soon realized that courting Zelda would be a great adventure. During his first visit to the Sayre house, she taunted her dignified father until, in a fit of rage, Judge Sayre chased her around the dinner table with a carving knife. Scott, who honed his own talent for provoking people during his years at Princeton, was certain he had found the love of his life.

Anxiously, they postponed their affair on October 26, 1918, when Scott's unit left Montgomery for Camp Mills on Long Island, New York. At Camp Mills, the unit prepared for the journey across the Atlantic and, finally, for combat. But on November 11, the warring nations signed an armistice. The United States' participation had broken the stalemate and ensured victory for the Allied powers. World War I ended.

Zelda Sayre was the Belle of Montgomery when
Scott Fitzgerald met her in 1918.

Unlike most Americans, Scott did not celebrate the peace. To
his great disappointment, he realized that he would never see
the European trenches and would never take part in any later
fighting. He had missed yet another chance for social advancement. However, in the short time he was stationed in the
Northeast, he did not miss any chances to prove his incompe-
tence as an officer. While his troops were unloading supplies at
a dock in Hoboken, New Jersey, he slipped away to visit
Princeton; thousands of dollars in goods were stolen during his
absence. Then, under even more mysterious circumstances, he

was found with a naked girl in a hotel room in Manhattan and put under military arrest.

After the armistice, Scott fought off his depression in a way that was becoming increasingly common for him: He drank himself into a stupor. He did not necessarily drink more alcohol than his friends and companions, many of whom suffered the effects of alcoholism. But small amounts of alcohol could dramatically change his personality. When his unit moved to Washington, D.C., and then again to Montgomery, he drank to fight off his frustration with his fruitless military service, his disappointment over Scribners' refusal to publish "The Romantic Egoist," and his depression after Father Fay's sudden death, of influenza, during a wartime diplomatic mission. He also drank to hide his intense anger and jealousy when Zelda insisted that he did not have a strong enough will, work ethic, or income potential to marry her. But as soon as he received his discharge in February 1919, he screwed up his courage and renewed his efforts to carve out a serious and successful future.

Dreaming of a life with Zelda and hoping to prove worthy of her hand in marriage, he ran to Manhattan to find work. He rented a dingy apartment on the upper east side of the city and took a job as a slogan writer for the Barron Collier advertising agency. He earned thirty-five dollars a week scribbling ads, and received 122 rejection slips for the stories and movie treatments he wrote at night. Despite such a rocky start to his new life, Scott remained confident that he would ultimately succeed in convincing Zelda to marry him. "EVERYTHING IS POSSIBLE," he told her in a telegram a few weeks after his discharge from Camp Sheridan. "I AM IN THE LAND OF AMBITION AND SUCCESS AND MY ONLY HOPE AND FAITH IS THAT MY DARLING HEART WILL BE WITH ME SOON."[8] But Scott's supreme optimism, and his enthusiasm for Manhattan, waned as his best efforts met with failure. He sold only one story during this first period in New York—"Babes in the Woods" appeared in *Smart Set*, a magazine edited by George Jean Nathan and the nation's preeminent cultural critic, H. L. Mencken—and it had been written during his years at Princeton. In June, during a visit to Montgomery, Zelda renewed her complaints about Scott's inadequacies and discontinued their relationship (even though he had already presented her with an engagement ring). Heartbroken, he retreated to alcohol and then, after quitting his job, to his family's house in St. Paul.

Rededicating himself to his novel, he worked quickly. He restructured much of the earlier manuscript and wrote entirely new chapters based on his recent courtship of Zelda Sayre. Under a new title, *This Side of Paradise*, an allusion to a line from a Rupert Brooke poem (". . .Well, this side of Paradise! . . ./ There's little comfort in the wise."), the story divided into two parts. The first section, "The Romantic Egotist," recounted the education of Amory Blaine, a sensitive, selfish child from St. Paul, Minnesota, who attends Princeton and then enlists in the army to fight in World War I. The second section, "The Education of a Personage," covered Blaine's first attempts at financial, social, and romantic success after the war. In the final version of *This Side of Paradise*, Scott knit together a patchwork of events from his life, from his courtship of Ginevra King— here called Isabelle Borgé—to his courtship of Zelda Sayre— here called Rosalind Connage. He excerpted entire passages from Father Fay's letters, Shane Leslie's letters, and Zelda's diaries. He incorporated sections of prose, verse, popular songs, and dramatic dialogue into the large, unwieldy structure of the novel. And he copied notations from his own diaries and snippets of dialogue from his conversations with John Peale Bishop, the model for Thomas Parke D'Invilliers, as well as other Princeton friends. Yet, somehow, Scott managed to create something more than a pastiche autobiography.

This Side of Paradise emerged as a bildungsroman, a novel about growing up, which Scott assembled from small fragments of experience. Throughout the novel Amory Blaine, like Scott himself, struggles to interpret the changing world in which he lives and to find a means to express those changes. "We're just one generation," D'Invilliers tells Blaine as they graduate from Princeton at the end of "The Romantic Egotist." "We're breaking all the links that seemed to bind us here to top-booted and high-stocked generations."[9] Blaine's generation of ambitious, somewhat lazy young men and flappers rebels against the moral conventions of the age. They drink hard liquor, they dance close together, they kiss in public, and they search for new ways to understand their experiences now that the old values—sobriety, hard work, and religious piety— seem outdated. Their new lifestyles free them from artificial restraints, but seem to promise disaster as well. "Wouldn't it be awful if this was—was the high point?" Blaine asks Rosalind near the end of the novel. "Beauty and love pass, I know . . . Oh, there's sadness too. I suppose all great happiness is a little sad."[10] After a series of harrowing, alcohol-induced experiences and nightmares, Blaine comes to fear his dissolute lifestyle and mourn his failures. At the end of the novel, he cries, "I know myself but that is all," and his words seem empty.[11] His future is just as uncertain as it was at the beginning.

Through the sheer force of his will, rather than some clear-eyed inspection of the social, political, and artistic challenges of his age, Scott wrote a novel that perfectly described his own generation of Americans. Bunny Wilson, always resentful that Scott, his intellectual inferior, could produce better and more insightful works of fiction, would later write that *This Side of Paradise* was "not really about anything; intellectually, it amounts to little more than a gesture—a gesture of infinite revolt."[12] But that sense of "infinite revolt" precisely captured the spirit of the nation's young, educated elite in 1919. It also captured Scott's most honest self-evaluation: the self-centered, alcoholic Blaine—who falls in love with the wrong women—seemed to predict Scott's own future. For these reasons, Scott's awkward, clumsy experimental novel worked. He sent his completed manuscript to Scribner's on September 3, 1919. On September 16, he received an acceptance letter from Max Perkins: "The book is so different that it is hard to prophesy how it will sell but we are all for taking a chance and supporting it with vigor."[13] Scott, however, expected big sales. He immediately left St. Paul, quitting a job he had just accepted at the Northern Pacific Railroad yard, and returned to New York to reap the benefits of his imminent stardom. Finally, at twenty-five years of age, he could call himself a professional writer. Most importantly, with the money from the novel and the status it conferred, he would be able to repair his relationship with Zelda.

Chapter 4

THE BEAUTIFUL

> The compensation of a very early success is a conviction
> that life is a romantic matter. In the best sense one stays
> young.
>
> —From "Early Success"[1]

Returning to New York in the fall of 1919, Scott found a literary agent to help him sell his short stories to the literary and popular magazines. And Harold Ober, who would open his own agency in 1929 but was working at Paul Reynolds when he met Scott, proved to be as true a friend and as loyal a business associate as Max Perkins. These two men, the agent and the editor, stayed with Scott until his death, encouraged him during the low points in his career, and kept him afloat financially. Scott, the unpredictable, unreliable talent, was lucky to have gained their support while he was still young, before he had an opportunity to abuse their trust. Of the two, Ober had the most immediate effect on Scott's life. Within weeks, he placed several of Scott's short stories in popular magazines, earning for Scott about $900 by the beginning of 1920. As with the early excerpts from *This Side of Paradise*, Mencken and Nathan continued to publish Scott's stories in their incisive literary journal, *Smart Set*. But now Scott was also attracting the interest of the high-paying, mass-circulation magazines such as *The Saturday Evening Post*, which paid $400 for "Head and Shoulders," a story about a child prodigy who devotes his life

to the study of modern philosophy until he meets an unedu-
cated showgirl, falls in love, quits college, and becomes a
vaudeville performer.

Scott was already boasting his new status as a professional writer but, with this sudden flood of cash, he started to live
the life he had always dreamed about. Clumsily stuffing money
into his pockets so that it was visible to the people he met, he
led his friends on a series of Christmastime escapades involving massive alcohol consumption and ruined hotel rooms, and
ending in his own nervous exhaustion. Earlier in 1919, the fed-
eral government had passed the Eighteenth Amendment to the
Constitution, outlawing the consumption of alcohol. Although
this amendment, commonly referred to as Prohibition, did not
take effect until January 1920, it had already changed the
complexion of American social life by the time Scott began his
holiday celebrations. Drinking became an adventure, an illegal
activity involving a mysterious underworld of bootleggers who
illegally manufactured alcohol and speakeasies that illegally
sold it. Prohibition, coinciding with his financial success, gave
Scott a vehicle for the unconventional and rebellious side of his
personality: In addition to hiding his insecurities, he would
now drink for attention, fame, glamour, and popularity.

But Scott's fast lifestyle sapped him physically and psy-
chologically. In January, he moved to New Orleans, hoping
that the warm, Southern climate would cure a cough he had
developed—he feared it might be an early stage of tuberculosis—and that the slower pace of Southern life would be more
conducive to serious, sustained literary work. He also hoped
that Zelda, in nearby Montgomery, would find it harder to
resist his marriage proposals if he could deliver them in person.
He continued to churn out short stories and began a new novel.
But the greatest success of his monthlong stay in New Orleans
came during his second visit to the Sayres' house. Zelda,
increasingly confident that Scott could provide her with a suit-
able lifestyle, announced their engagement. Though they were
Episcopalians, the Sayres consented to the marriage. Minnie
Sayre expressed more concern over Zelda's erratic behavior
than Scott's Catholicism: "A good Catholic is as good as any

Beer flowed freely through the streets—and down into the
gutters—during Prohibition.

other man and that is good enough. It will take more than the
Pope to make Zelda good: you will have to call on God
Almighty direct."[2]

Scott returned to New York in early February to await
Zelda. Again battling concerns that Scott could not satisfy her,
she was reluctant to leave her old life of parties and fawning
college boys for a new life as the wife of an almost-famous writer. On the 24th, Scott wired her in Montgomery with more
good news: "I HAVE SOLD THE MOVIE RIGHTS OF
HEAD AND SHOULDERS TO THE METRO COMPA-
NY FOR TWENTY FIVE HUNDRED DOLLARS I
LOVE YOU DEAREST GIRL."[3] And then, in late March,
This Side of Paradise was published to generally rave reviews.
The New York Times Literary Supplement called the novel
"tiresome" with dialogue "artificial beyond belief." *America*,
objecting to the immorality of the novel's hard-drinking, sexu-
ally adventurous college students, declared, "If the parties to

Amory's various love-affairs are faithful portraits of the modern American girl, the country is going to the dogs rapidly." But H.L. Mencken, the most influential critic in the nation, called Scott "an artist—an apt and delicate weaver of words, a clever hand, a sound workman" who wrote with "a brilliancy that is as rare in American writing as honesty is in American statecraft."[4] And the American public, drawn to Scott's depictions of the flappers and their beaux, responded with even greater enthusiasm to *This Side of Paradise* than Mencken, buying up the first printing in 24 hours and 50,000 copies by the end of 1920. Suddenly a major figure in both literary and show-business circles—Metro produced *The Chorus Girl's Romance*, a movie based on "Head and Shoulders," later in 1920—Scott took New York by storm. But Zelda held out until he returned to Montgomery and coaxed her to join him in Manhattan by April 3 for an Easter afternoon wedding at the rectory of St. Patrick's Cathedral.

Almost immediately after the wedding, Scott and Zelda began shaping their New York personae. They honeymooned at the Biltmore and Commodore hotels in New York, and built their reputations for bad behavior. Upon arriving at the Commodore—after an irate manager expelled them from the Biltmore for disturbing the hotel's other patrons—they spun in the hotel's revolving door for a half hour. They disrupted theater performances by deliberately laughing at inappropriate times. They visited Cottage at Princeton, where Scott introduced Zelda as his mistress, suffered a black eye during a brawl, and earned himself a club suspension. (Cottage expelled him later in the year when he returned dressed as the Greek god Apollo, playing a shepherd's pipe; his behavior, coupled with his depiction of Princeton in *This Side of Paradise*, had offended the wrong people.) While Scott and Zelda wreaked havoc on polite society, they cultivated a new style, mingling their unconventional party antics with genteel tastes in clothing, art, and conversation. Scott enlisted the help of Midge Hersey, the friend who introduced him to Ginevra King, to improve Zelda's outdated, provincial wardrobe. And Zelda was a quick study. Soon, as the prototypical flapper, she would be setting the fashions for others to follow. Not long after the wedding, a

Scott and Zelda, shown here in 1921, made their mark on New York society with their unique brand of madcap elegance.

depiction of Zelda dancing in the fountain outside the exclusive Plaza Hotel appeared at the center of an illustrated stage curtain at the Greenwich Village Follies. Young, beautiful, and unstable, she took center stage in Manhattan's high society on the eve of an economic boom and a cultural explosion. And Scott appointed himself chronicler of the decade of prosperity, freedom, and, above all, fun, that he would rename the Jazz Age. "America was going on the greatest, gaudiest spree in history," he remembered years later, "and there was going to be plenty to tell about it."[5]

In the summer of 1920, the Fitzgeralds moved into a beach cottage in Westport, Connecticut, where they hosted a series of riotous parties and argued with each other incessantly. Zelda craved Scott's attention and would act outrageously to get it. The suburbs proved too quiet for her when Scott was working, so she seldom allowed him to work uninterrupted. Even during their first months together, it was obvious that Zelda would not be content in the conventional female roles of wife and supporter. She wanted to live on her own terms and taste her own success. So they left Westport at the end of the summer and rented an apartment at 38 West Fifty-ninth Street, and then at 381 East Fifty-ninth Street, in Manhattan. While Scott worked diligently on his novel, Zelda met with friends and spent money lavishly. In August, Scribner's published a volume of Scott's short stories, *Flappers and Philosophers*, to capitalize on the popularity of his first novel, beginning a publishing pattern the firm would try to maintain throughout Scott's career. But even the advance from that volume, combined with the extraordinary sums Scott had earned during the previous year, could not keep the couple out of debt. Zelda's spending, Scott's drinking, and the delay in income while he finished his novel eliminated their savings. "I'm at my wit's end," Scott wrote to Max Perkins at the end of 1920. "Isn't there some way you could regard this as an advance on the new novel rather than on the Xmas sale which won't be due me till July? . . . I need $1600.00."[6]

The Fitzgeralds' financial concerns took on an even more serious cast in February 1921, when Zelda announced that she was pregnant. Yet they chose to maintain their adventurous, expensive lifestyle as long as they could. They had been planning to visit Europe when Scott finished his new novel; now, with a child on the way who would surely require more of their time and attention, they knew they could not wait that long. On borrowed money, they booked two berths on the ocean liner *Aquitania* and, in May, set sail for England. In London, Shane Leslie led them on a tour and invited them to dinner with his first cousin, Winston Churchill, head of the British Colonial Office and future prime minister. They raced through museums and historical sites—in which they had little interest—visited Oxford, the ancient college town, bought expensive English clothing, and then moved on to Paris, Venice, Florence, and Rome. By July 9, Zelda was exhausted from the constant travel and Scott was disappointed with the Europeans' poor response to his writing, including *This Side of Paradise*. Since neither was particularly comfortable living in a foreign culture, they cut their trip short and returned to New York.

Deciding that their child would be born among familiar surroundings, they rented a house in Dellwood, Minnesota, on White Bear Lake outside St. Paul. There, Scott finished editing his second novel, *The Beautiful and Damned*. In September, excerpts from the novel appeared in *Metropolitan Magazine*. To Scott's disappointment, the magazine's editors cut a quarter of the total words before printing their serialized version, reducing a detailed novel about New York society into a much less interesting story of a troubled marriage. Seeing the flaws of his novel more clearly after this *Metropolitan Magazine* debacle, Scott undertook another series of revisions.

On October 26, just as Scott completed his final revisions of *The Beautiful and Damned*, Zelda gave birth to a girl, Frances Scott Fitzgerald, forever known as "Scottie." Scottie would be the Fitzgeralds' only child. (In later years, Zelda would have three abortions. And in 1930, an ovarian infection would make it impossible for her to conceive again.) From the beginning, Scottie confused and troubled her irresponsible parents. "I hope it's beautiful and a fool . . . a beautiful little fool," Zelda said moments after Scottie's birth.[7] The demands of parenthood dampened their social lives and nearly overshadowed the publication of Scott's second novel. Seeking his family's support, they moved into a house near Summit Avenue in St. Paul. There, through the late fall and winter of 1921, Scott tried to write a play and Zelda tried to learn the secrets of motherhood. Compared to their previous adventures in New York, their new routine as parents in St. Paul seemed dull and uninspiring.

The Beautiful and Damned finally appeared in bookstores in March 1922. The story of Anthony Patch, a Harvard graduate who aspires to a life of leisure, and his equally stylish and superficial wife Gloria, the novel fictionalizes Scott's relationship with Zelda—including their year in the Connecticut suburbs—and, like *Tender Is the Night*, predicts their troubled future. In the beginning, Patch believes that he will inherit his wealthy grandfather's fortunes. He therefore refuses to "submit to mediocrity, to go to work."[8] At the same time, Gloria, "the most living person he had ever seen," reinforces Patch's laziness and irresponsibility.[9] "Everything I do," she tells him, "is in accordance with my ideas: to use every minute of these years, when I'm young, in having the best time I possibly can."[10] For a while, they are able to enjoy a glamorous, carefree existence. But after his grandfather discovers that he has been wasting his time on three-day parties and illegal liquor, Patch loses his inheritance. Under pressure to maintain his lifestyle, his self-respect, and Gloria's happiness, Patch loses his grip on reality. At the conclusion of the novel, after years of court battles during which he contests his grandfather's will, Patch regains his inheritance but suffers a mental breakdown in the process. Friendless, an object of scorn, he stands at the rail of a ship bound for Europe, mumbling, "I showed them . . . It was a hard fight, but I didn't give up and I came through."[11]

Scott's Princeton friends John Peale Bishop and Bunny Wilson summed up the critics' response to his latest effort. In the New York *Herald*, Bishop wrote, "Stylistically speaking, it is not so well written, neither is it so carelessly written . . . Fitzgerald is at the moment of announcing the meaninglessness of life magnificently alive."[12] Wilson, writing for *Bookman*, also noted that the novel "makes an advance over *This Side of Paradise*," though it remained an "imperfect" piece as a whole.[13]

Most critics noted Fitzgerald's failure to write in a consistent voice; he seemed to alternate between the wry, sarcastic style of H.L. Mencken and his own, delicately romantic prose without bringing the two together. But in a review for the *New York Tribune* entitled "Friend Husband's Latest," her first published piece, Zelda sarcastically evaded any questions about the book's literary quality and noted its popular appeal: "Its value as a manual of etiquette is incalculable. Where could you get a better example of how not to behave than from the adventures of Gloria?"[14] Zelda, of course, knew that Gloria's behavior (and her own) was precisely the novel's greatest selling point; flappers were still making news. She also noted that Scott had lifted entire passages out of her own diary and inserted them into the novel. "Plagiarism begins at home," she joked.[15] With the publication of *The Beautiful and Damned*, Zelda clearly emerged as the most important influence on Scott's life and work; she was his inspiration, his primary subject matter, his collaborator and, with increasing frequency, his adversary. Together, they lived their lives in a way that intrigued the reading public. As long as Scott could find the time and energy to continue writing, and as long as he could translate his experiences with Zelda into fiction, they would survive and thrive.

Scribner's sold more than forty thousand copies of *The Beautiful and Damned* during its first year of publication, though Scott remained in debt to his publisher until he sold the movie rights to both *This Side of Paradise* and *The Beautiful and Damned* for a combined profit of $12,500. But by the time his second collection of short stories, *Tales of the Jazz Age*, appeared in September 1922, Scott seemed to have reclaimed his position as the preeminent writer of his generation. With two acclaimed novels and a handful of important short stories—including "The Ice Palace" and "Bernice Bobs Her Hair" from *Flappers and Philosophers*, and "May Day" and "The Diamond as Big as the Ritz" from *Tales of the Jazz Age*—he had already amassed a significant body of work. And his finest work was ahead of him.

Chapter 5

PINNACLE

He had come a long way to this blue lawn, and his dream
must have seemed so close that he could hardly fail to
grasp it. He did not know that it was already behind him.
—From *The Great Gatsby*[1]

In the fall of 1922, the Fitzgeralds left the relative calm of
Minnesota to return, once again, to New York, a city they
were helping to define. They rented a house on the northern
shore of Long Island, in the town of Great Neck. Beyond the
New York City limits, beyond the dirt and congestion of urban
life, but close enough to Manhattan to afford its residents an
easy commute, Great Neck attracted some of the most famous
and powerful people in the nation. World War I general John
Pershing, Broadway producer George M. Cohan, comedian
Groucho Marx, polo star Tommy Hickock, actor Basil Rath-
bone, and a host of others gathered in Great Neck in the early
twenties. Enormous, luxurious mansions dotted the town's
waterfront property along Manhasset Bay. By day, they were
the stately homes of the New York elite; by night, they were the
sites of elaborate, riotous parties where bootlegged liquor ran
freely and full orchestras played dance music into the wee
hours of the morning. If Scott Fitzgerald believed that living in
the suburbs would be good for his writing, he was right. Great
Neck provided him with a wealth of material for his future stories. But he accomplished very little while he was living there;
the lure of the parties, and of the alcohol, was too strong.

Though Scott was the most notorious drinker in New York—as the man most likely to lose control of himself when drunk—he was now traveling in social circles that relied on alcohol to provide entertainment, a means of communication, and release. Despite Prohibition, liquor consumption remained the focal point of the Great Neck community. And Scott fell victim to that lifestyle almost immediately. His best friend during this period, the journalist and story writer Ring Lardner, was quieter and more dignified when drunk; yet Lardner's own alcoholism only reinforced Scott's increasing dependency. Together, they shared literary ideas—Scott would compile and entitle Lardner's brilliant 1924 collection of stories, *How to Write Short Stories (with Examples)*—and several hilarious adventures, including a midnight dance on publisher Frank Doubleday's front lawn in an attempt to attract the attention of their literary hero, novelist Joseph Conrad, who was staying with Doubleday. However, Ring and Scott pushed each other along a tragic path; their alcoholism would weaken their literary output, destroy their families, and shorten their lives.

Within the New York literary community, Fitzgerald became a divisive figure. Some writers, like Lardner and John Dos Passos, the brilliant, young novelist and social commentator, enjoyed Scott's company and respected his work—though Dos Passos, like many of Scott's friends, distrusted Zelda, who seemed generally unstable.[2] Others, particularly those of the previous generation, such as Theodore Dreiser, Edith Wharton, and Sherwood Anderson, found him childish and, when he was drinking, undignified. Scott, who shared his father's respect for genteel manners and respectability, was now living on the edge of vulgarity. Struggling to pay his debts to Scribner's and Harold Ober, he wrote a series of second-rate stories for the popular magazines. With the money from these stories, he was able to maintain a lifestyle that included a second-hand Rolls Royce and an endless stream of visitors and companions all searching for the high life that Scott and Zelda had made famous. But even as Scott's life took on the character of an endless hangover, and even as his reputation within New York's elite community suffered, his fame grew throughout the rest of the nation. He and Zelda appeared on the cover of *Hearst's*

International in May 1923, in a photograph that would be reprinted countless times in other magazines and newspapers during the twenties. Holding hands, staring directly at the camera, serious and elegant, they were still the public's ideal young couple.

Scott knew his fame would not last, however, if he did not continue to produce first-rate work. So that spring, bolstered by Bunny Wilson's praise and encouragement, he published the play he had started writing while he was still living in Minnesota. Titled *The Vegetable, or From President to Postman*, it was a Menckenesque satire of American society in which a railroad clerk wakes from a drunken stupor to find that he has been nominated for president. As he had proven in the weaker passages of *The Beautiful and Damned*, Scott simply was not equipped to be a political satirist; he wrote best when he wrote about romance and dreams. In *The Vegetable*, which turns out to have been the railroad clerk's dream all along—he eventually becomes a postman, not a president—Scott failed once again to blend these conflicting themes into a unified work. Despite Wilson's endorsement, critics lambasted the play. When it opened on November 10, 1923, at Nixon's Apollo Theater in Atlantic City, New Jersey, many of the audience members walked out early. It ran for a mere week before the producers closed it for good.

By the end of the year, having suffered a major failure with *The Vegetable*, Scott found himself $5,000 in debt. He had earned $36,000 in 1923 and somehow spent it all—once again, his friends blamed Zelda. Characteristically, he stopped drinking, locked himself in his Great Neck garage, and wrote magazine stories until he paid off what he owed. In April, he wrote a letter to Max Perkins containing as honest an assessment of his recent failures as he could possibly conceive:

> The last four months of course I've worked but in the two years—over two years—before that, I produced exactly *one* play, *half a dozen* short stories and three or four articles—an average of about *one hundred* words a day. If I'd spent this time reading or traveling or doing anything—even staying healthy—it'd be different but I

spent it uselessly, neither in study nor in contemplation but only in drinking and raising hell generally.[3]

He cited three particularly bad habits he wished to eliminate: "laziness," "referring everything to Zelda," and "word consciousness." Writing, which had once been an easy process for Scott, and the one aspect of his life that was unimpeded by his often crippling self-doubts, had become a difficult, nerve-wracking process. He needed to mend his ways and change his outlook if he were going to revive his career. And, as usual, he associated the rebirth of his career with a change in scenery. In May 1924, he, Zelda, and Scottie left Great Neck for Paris.

He disliked the City of Lights during his first visit three years earlier. But Paris offered a lower cost of living and greater cultural freedom than most American cities, and it became a center for American artists and writers in the mid-twenties. Anyone who wished to experiment with new artistic or literary techniques, or who tired of Prohibition-era restraints on drinking and entertainment, could find a community of like-minded Americans in the cafés and inexpensive apartments in the city's Montparnasse quarter. The Fitzgeralds never fully joined this vibrant expatriate culture. Neither Scott nor Zelda would ever be satisfied with the low-budget lifestyle of the Left Bank. And Scott had already developed his literary style and reputation before arriving in Europe. Although he was a member of the same generation as the High Modernist writers—including the novelists James Joyce, William Faulkner, and Ernest Hemingway, all of whom lived in Paris during the twenties—he had solidified his reputation earlier in the decade, and wrote in a less experimental style. Thus, he remained an outsider in Montparnasse, even though he would soon claim the most important expatriates as friends.

Few expatriates would have as great an impact on his life as Gerald and Sara Murphy. Almost as soon as they met, Scott considered Gerald a hero. Heir to his father's Fifth Avenue leather goods shop, Gerald had graduated from Yale, blazed Manhattan's high society, married his high school sweetheart Sara Wiborg, a debutante from Cincinnati, and then set sail for France in 1915 in order to study painting in the same art

During the 1925 holiday season, the Fitzgeralds frolic
together in their Paris apartment.

community that supported Pablo Picasso, Georges Braque, and the Cubists. He developed into a capable, if not important, painter. But by 1924, he and Sara occupied the center of an important social and artistic circle that included composer Cole Porter, poet Archibald MacLeish, novelists John Dos Passos and Ernest Hemingway, and Picasso. The Murphys' generosity, hospitality, and support sustained each of these figures during one of the most remarkable creative explosions of the twentieth century. And each summer, they hosted an odd but exciting assortment of characters at the Villa America, their house in Antibes on the French Riviera.

During their first summer in Europe, Scott, Zelda, Scottie, and Scottie's English Nanny, Miss Maddock, followed the Murphys to the Riviera and rented Villa Marie near St. Raphaël. There, when he was not drinking excessively and disrupting the Murphys' otherwise dignified parties (he would deliberately smash their wine glasses or roll on the floor whining, "You all like Zelda better than me"[4]), Scott worked furiously on a new novel. "I think my novel is about the best American novel ever written," he wrote to Max Perkins in late August.[5] Despite the comfort and confidence he derived from his work, however, the summer of 1924 ushered in one of the most difficult periods in his life. As he rededicated his energies to writing and tried to compensate for his most recent literary failures, Zelda sought her entertainment elsewhere. She flirted with the aviators from a nearby French naval base, just as she had flirted with the soldiers from Camp Sheridan and Camp Taylor in Montgomery. Inevitably, she fell in love with a handsome aviator and future vice admiral named Edouard Josanne, who would fly stunts over the Villa Marie to attract her attention. Josanne was reassigned to a different base in midsummer, but not before Zelda confessed her infidelities to Scott. Her short-lived affair with Josanne prompted the most serious crisis in the Fitzgeralds' already tumultuous marriage. Somehow, they salvaged their marriage after a series of dramatic, and often public, arguments. But neither was ever the same. Heartbroken and guilt ridden, Zelda slowly began to change; her charming unpredictability took an ominous, even dangerous, turn that worried her friends. She even attempted suicide by ingesting a large dose of sleeping pills. Scott coped by devoting his remaining energies to his novel. And both hid their difficulties by drinking even more heavily than before. When their five-month lease expired in November, they left the Riviera for Rome.

While living at the exclusive Piazza di Spagna hotel at the foot of the Spanish Steps—close to the house where Fitzgerald's favorite Romantic poet, John Keats, once lived—Scott revised the proofs of his new novel and recuperated from a severe flu that had been aggravated by his increasing dependence on alcohol. Zelda also contracted a mysterious illness during that cold, damp winter; she experienced abdominal pains for the next several months, as doctors disagreed on a diagnosis. But the worst came on a cold night in January when Scott, emboldened by drink, argued with a taxi driver over a cab fare. As he shouted at the driver, another man interfered in the quarrel. Scott punched this second man to the ground before learning that he had hit a plainclothes policeman. Arrested for assaulting an officer, Scott spent the night at a police station. As Zelda tried to gather enough money to pay bail, Scott was beaten and humiliated by the Italian officers. After this harrowing experience, the Fitzgeralds left Rome.

They toured southern Italy before settling on the island of Capri in the Bay of Naples. In that warm, sunny climate, Zelda taught herself to paint and Scott finished revising the new novel. On February 18, 1925, he finally mailed the completed manuscript to Max Perkins with a note attached: "After six weeks of uninterrupted work the proof is finished and the last of it goes to you this afternoon. On the whole its been very successful labor." The note then lists the five most important changes he made to the novel Max had first seen the previous October. Topping the list: "I've brought Gatsby to life."[6]

During the ensuing weeks, Scott seemed most concerned about the title of his new novel, *The Great Gatsby*. He suggested several alternatives including "Trimalchio in West Egg"— alluding to a famous party-giver from Roman literature—and "Under the Red, White and Blue," but Max Perkins convinced him to stick with his first choice. In November, Perkins had already called the manuscript version of *Gatsby* "a wonder" with "vitality to an extraordinary degree, and *glamour,* and a great deal of underlying thought of unusual quality."[7] Now that Scott had corrected minor errors and clarified a few scenes, it seemed a masterpiece. With *The Great Gatsby,* Scott proved that he had developed as a writer in spite of his careless lifestyle and troubled marriage. If *This Side of Paradise* and *The Beautiful and Damned* had been sprawling collections of loosely connected scenes, *Gatsby* was their exact opposite: a short, finely crafted, sharp novel. Late in 1924, Scott admitted that he was trying to compose "the best American novel ever written," and he expertly manipulated every element of *Gatsby*—its pace, imagery, characters and dialogue—toward that end.[8]

Ingeniously, Scott adopted a new narrative mode, adapted from the novels of Joseph Conrad, in order to tell his story. The novel's narrator, Nick Carraway, is not its dramatic focus. As a Midwesterner who works on Wall Street and lives in a fictional Long Island town called West Egg, Carraway is an outsider who shares his audience's wonder at the people he describes. But he also develops into an able critic of the events he observes.

Like most Americans, Carraway aspires to live a more extravagant, more comfortable, more romantic lifestyle. He finds his ideal in a mysterious neighbor, a man named Gatsby who hosts lavish parties that attract hundreds of people and continue into the early hours of the morning. "People were not invited," Carraway says of Gatsby's first parties. "They went there. They got into automobiles which bore them out to Long Island, and somehow they ended up at Gatsby's door . . . Sometimes they came and went without having met Gatsby at all, came for the party with a simplicity of heart that was its own ticket of admission."[9] In time, Carraway learns that the parties are nothing more than an elaborate ploy to attract the attention of a single woman, Daisy Buchanan. Daisy, Carraway's cousin, lives with her crude, aristocratic husband, Tom Buchanan, in a mansion in the more exclusive town of East Egg (modeled on the Fitzgeralds' own Great Neck). As Buchanan's wife, she enjoys a life of endless leisure, and even boredom. But once she was Gatsby's first love. And Gatsby, Carraway learns, has worked his entire life to earn enough money and amass enough prestige to win her back. Carraway sees the futility of Gatsby's dream; Daisy will never leave her rich and powerful husband for Gatsby, who might have made his money through illegal activities. Even worse, she is selfish and coldhearted and may not be worth the effort. "There must have been moments even that afternoon when Daisy tumbled short of his dreams," Carraway says as he recounts the events of the final meeting between Gatsby and Daisy. "Not through her own fault, but because of the colossal vitality of his illusion. It had gone beyond her, beyond everything."[10] In the end, Gatsby's dream collapses in a horrific spiral of violence, and Carraway leaves New York, a place he comes to associate with cruelty and broken hearts.

Beyond the simple story of love and loyalty, *The Great Gatsby* is what Scott intended it to be, a novel of explicitly American themes. Gatsby lives a mythological life; he is a self-made man, rising from rags to riches. Born Jimmy Gatz from North Dakota, he leaves home, changes his name, and re-creates himself as a suburban gentleman. He derives influence from his newfound wealth and believes that his money gives him access to Daisy Buchanan's elitist world. He even tells Carraway that Daisy's voice "is full of money," as if she were the ultimate trophy, the ultimate proof of his success.[11] He does not realize that he cannot buy social standing, business affiliations, or family ties; and he does not realize that, without these things, he cannot have Daisy. The tragedy of the novel, then, is the tragedy of the self-made man: There are some limits that he cannot exceed, no matter how hard he works.

In addition to this broad theme, *The Great Gatsby* offers a stinging critique of the New York elite. At the end of the novel, Carraway calls the Buchanans "a rotten crowd" and says that Gatsby, who lies about his past and hides his involvement in the Manhattan underworld, is "worth the whole damn bunch put together."[12] To Carraway—and to Fitzgerald—the Buchanans' selfishness, their lack of concern for those who cannot be accepted into their social circle, merely echoes a more general immorality among the very wealthy. The novel judges elite society and finds it guilty of a criminal negligence toward the rest of the world. To emphasize this theme of moral judgment, Fitzgerald introduces the most distinct image of the novel: a pair of eyes painted onto a billboard and staring down at the highway between East Egg and Manhattan. Once the eyes of an oculist, Doctor T. J. Eckleburg, they assume a variety of meanings in the course of the novel's action. Near the end, after the Gatsby-Buchanan love triangle produces its first violent tragedy, they even assume a religious significance: "God sees everything," one character observes as he stares at the billboard.[13]

By skillfully weaving these strands of social criticism and moral judgment throughout his novel, Scott produced a fiction that was fast-paced, entertaining, and important. Writers praised *The Great Gatsby* as one of the truly original novels of the era, and praised Scott for his almost musical skill with the English language. T. S. Eliot—the writer whose most important poem, "The Wasteland," influenced Scott's depiction of T. J. Eckleberg—wrote that *Gatsby* "interested and excited" him more than any novel he had seen in years. "It seems to me to be the first step that American fiction has taken since Henry James," he concluded.[14] Bunny Wilson told Scott it was "the best thing you have done—the best planned, the best sustained, the best written."[15] Even the normally reserved matriarch of the Paris expatriates, Gertrude Stein, praised Scott for "creating the contemporary world much as Thackery did in his *Pendennis* and *Vanity Fair* and this isn't a bad compliment."[16] The book critics generally agreed with these writers' assessments when *Gatsby* appeared in stores in April 1925. Only the reading public seemed to disagree. Perhaps, with the author now living in Europe, Scribner's could not market the book as easily as Scott's previous works. Or perhaps the flapper and the Jazz Age party life had fallen out of fashion. For whatever reason, the public bought only 20,000 copies of *The Great Gatsby*, far fewer than they bought of his previous books. A theater adaptation opened in New York in 1926 and ran for 112 shows, and Hollywood soon bought the movie rights. From these subsidiary contracts, Scott earned an extra $35,000, an enormous sum.

But the money he earned from the sales of the book itself could not sustain his family, his wife's extravagant tastes, or his drinking habit. When the theater and movie money ran out, he would have to continue writing the formulaic short stories that the public had come to expect.

In *The Great Gatsby*, Scott finally produced the brilliant novel he had always aspired to write. Yet, after it was published, he was forced to swallow a bitter irony: He could capture an entire nation's attention with inferior, hastily composed work, but he could not find a readership for the one novel that would solidify his reputation as a master of American fiction.

A movie still from the 1926 Paramount silent picture,
The Great Gatsby

Chapter 6

THE DAMNED

He was not really disappointed to find Paris was so
empty. But the stillness in the Ritz bar was strange and
portentous. It was not an American bar any more.
—From "Babylon Revisited"[1]

s Scott's career declined after the publication of *The Great
Gatsby*, another writer emerged to claim Scott's mantel as
the spokesman for the "Lost Generation," the disillusioned
Americans who came of age during World War I. Unlike Scott,
this new literary giant, Ernest Hemingway, participated in the
combat in Europe and was seriously wounded. He served as an
ambulance driver for the Red Cross, not as a soldier, but earned
medals for bravery and returned to his hometown of Oak Park,
Illinois, a war hero. Forgoing a college education, Hemingway
learned to write as a reporter for the *Kansas City Star* and the
Toronto *Sun*. In 1921, he moved to Paris as a foreign corre-
spondent for the *Sun*. By that time, he had decided to stake his
future on his fiction. Presenting himself as a self-confident,
athletic artist, the twenty-one-year-old Hemingway thrust
himself into the center of the expatriate community. He studied new, Modernist writing techniques pioneered by the poet
Ezra Pound and the versatile patron of the arts, Gertrude
Stein. And both Pound and Stein encouraged him to develop a
distinctive, unadorned writing style based on short, declarative
sentences. Unlike Scott, who achieved literary fame quickly,
Hemingway labored for years in Paris, a poor writer whose

name was known only among the expatriates. In 1925, the publisher Boni and Liveright finally introduced Hemingway's work to the U.S. audience; when the short story collection *In Our Time* appeared, reviewers announced the birth of a major new voice in American letters.

Scott may have doubted his own writing ability from time to time, and his personal insecurities may have been severe, but he always tried to help writers whose talent he admired. Just as he had assisted, and even carried, Ring Lardner through the publication of *How to Write Short Stories*, he championed Hemingway to his editor at Scribner's, Max Perkins. "This is to tell you about a young man named Ernest Hemmingway [sic], who lives in Paris, (an American) writes for the transatlantic Review + has a brilliant future," he wrote to Perkins in October 1924. "Ezra Pound published a collection of his short pieces in Paris . . . "I haven't it heard now but it's remarkable + I'd look him up right away. He's the real thing."[2] Scott's letter led to one of the most profitable writer/editor relationships in American literary history. Perkins agreed to publish Hemingway's next two books, *The Sun Also Rises* (about which Scott offered several useful editorial suggestions) and *The Torrents of Spring*, and every subsequent book in a career that, like Scott's, helped to define American culture in the twentieth century. But Scott did not actually meet Hemingway until June 1925. The two finally crossed paths in a bar called Le Dingo. Drunk and effusive, as he usually was when introduced to writers he admired, Scott declared his admiration for Hemingway's work. Then he passed out and had to be escorted home. The scene annoyed Hemingway, who prided himself on his ability to drink without losing control. From that moment, despite Scott's generosity in advancing Hemingway's career, Hemingway would treat Scott with a mixture of brotherly concern and contempt. He would belittle Scott, privately and publicly, prey on his insecurities, and create unflattering portraits of him for a reading public fascinated by their legendary friendship. "Scott was a man then who looked like a boy with a face between handsome and pretty," he would write in *A Moveable Feast*, his posthumously published account of expatriate life. "The mouth worried you until you knew him and then it worried you more."[3] This passage, both feminizing Scott and reducing him to a child, exemplified Hemingway's typical critique of his friend. He mocked Scott in order to make himself appear tougher, more masculine, and superior. In return, Scott's admiration for Hemingway bordered on hero-worship and did not diminish with time. To Scott, Hemingway seemed to embody every quality he lacked: physical strength, courage, self-discipline, and a commanding presence (his friends would soon call the fatherlike Hemingway "Papa"). But Hemingway did not fool Zelda, who saw through his rugged persona and called him "bogus."[4]

Scott was not the only target of Hemingway's scorn. In time, Hemingway would reject all the people who helped him

A dapper Ernest Hemingway, Paris 1924

become the most famous literary personality of the era, including Sherwood Anderson, his early mentor, and Gertrude Stein. But in 1925, he was still a favorite among the older writers and artists in Paris, and introduced Scott to many of the more important figures in the expatriate community, including Stein herself. Having settled in the city in 1903, Stein was one of the first Americans to champion Paris's artistic culture. Her published works, including her 1909 story collection *Three Lives* and *Tender Buttons*, a volume of experimental poetry, earned the praise of other writers but made little impact on the reading public. Instead of her writing, she become famous for the artistic salon she and her lifelong companion, Alice B. Toklas, hosted in their apartment at 27 rue de Fleurus. She collected the paintings of Paul Cézanne and Pierre Bonnard long before their reputations were established with most critics. She supported the Cubist revolution in pictorial art. And she prided herself on her ability to identify young talent. Henri Matisse and Pablo Picasso visited her frequently, as did Hemingway, Sherwood Anderson, and poet William Carlos Williams. She liked Scott immediately. Unlike most writers Scott met, Stein appreciated his exaggerated flatteries. And she returned them in her 1933 book, *The Autobiography of Alice B. Toklas*: "She thinks Fitzgerald will be read when many of his well-known contemporaries are forgotten."[5] Unfortunately, Stein paid less attention to Zelda, who always found herself seated beside the quiet, less interesting Toklas. As a result of such snubs, Zelda's resentment grew; she was tiring of her role as the wife of a famous writer and began searching for her own vehicle for self-expression. She had taken up painting in Capri; now she was looking for something new to occupy her time.

In the late summer of 1925—after Scott completed "The Rich Boy," his novella about a wealthy, spoiled man's inability to find love—the Fitzgeralds spent a month with the Murphys in Antibes, where they also vacationed with John Dos Passos, poet Archibald MacLeish, actor Rudolph Valentino, and Italy's former premier Vittorio Orlando, among other celebrities. Then they traveled to England, but Scott disliked the country even more during this second visit, particularly after learning that his books sold poorly there and that his English publisher, William Collins, refused to publish *The Great Gatsby*. By January 1926, they were moving again. This time, they stopped in the French Pyrenees, in a village called Salies-de Béarn, where Zelda received treatment for colitis as well as for gynecological complications possibly resulting from her abortions (Parisian doctors would remove her appendix in June, but she continued to experience abdominal pain). In March, they returned to the Murphys in Antibes and nearly wore out their welcome. As

The exuberant couple prepare for a stroll on
the Riviera, 1926.

always, they drank too much alcohol and acted outrageously. When they were not invited to one of the Murphys' parties, they responded by throwing garbage over the fence surrounding the Villa America. On a separate occasion, Scott tried to run over Zelda with a car as she goaded him on. And Zelda, who had already tried to commit suicide once, threw herself down a flight of stairs when she noticed Scott fawning over the dancer Isadora Duncan. The Murphys resorted to extreme measures to deal with their unruly guest: They banished Scott from the Villa America for three weeks.

Such crises were becoming more common now, as Scott's alcoholism came to dominate his personality and Zelda's physical and mental health declined. After each lapse in judgment, Scott agonized over his behavior and frequently apologized to the people he offended. "I was quite ashamed of the other morning," he wrote to Hemingway in a note apologizing for an unannounced, early morning visit to Hemingway's apartment. "However it is only fair to say that the deplorable man who entered your apartment *was not* me but a man named Johnston who has often been mistaken for me."[6] Despite his good humor, however, Scott recognized that his and Zelda's problems were finally affecting his work: He failed to publish a single new story between February 1926 and June 1927.[7]

Fortunately, Scribner's published another volume of his short stories, *All the Sad Young Men*, in February 1926 in order to capitalize on Scott's post-*Gatsby* publicity. The volume included "The Rich Boy" and "Absolution," a story that Scott had first included in *The Great Gatsby* as Jay Gatsby's biography, but cut during the editing process. Scribner's sold more than sixteen thousand copies, fewer than they sold of *Gatsby*. But, when the profits were added to Scott's income for the play and movie versions of *Gatsby*, it earned the Fitzgeralds enough to sustain their increasingly wasteful lifestyle through another season. Although the majority of the collected stories were drawn from Scott's lesser magazine work, reviewers generally praised *All the Sad Young Men*. Still, two noteworthy observations appeared among the reviewers' comments. First, they compared the book unfavorably to Hemingway's *In Our*

Time—a fact that only reinforced Scott's admiration for the younger writer. Second, they noted that Scott's commercial concerns, his willingness to publish inferior work in order to make money, was detracting from his overall output. It seemed to many that he had compromised his literary standards.[8]

But the reality of Scott's situation was even worse than the critics imagined: He simply could not write anymore. He had begun a new novel in 1924, shortly after finishing *Gatsby*, but made little progress on it during the ensuing years. His drinking, Zelda's deteriorating mental health, and their almost constant fighting had reduced him to a mere shell of the writer he had been. He arranged for a complete retreat at the end of 1926. In December, he, Zelda, and Scottie boarded the SS *Conte Biancamano* in Genoa, Italy, and returned to the United States. From the ship, he wrote a brief letter to Hemingway that served as a desperate prayer for the future:

> I can't tell you how much your friendship has meant to me during this year and a half—it is the brightest thing in our trip to Europe for me . . . I go back with my novel still unfinished and with less health + not much more money than when I came, but somehow content, for the moment, with motion and New York ahead and Zelda's entire recovery—and happy about the amount of my book that I've already written.[9]

Sadly, Scott's optimism in Zelda's recovery and in his own writing ability was unfounded. Only thirty years old, he had already achieved great fame and then fallen from public favor, developed a severe alcohol dependency, witnessed his wife's slow collapse, and lost the intense desire for prestige that had driven him since the earliest days of childhood. Worst of all, he was not sure if his life had reached rock bottom, or if he had farther to fall. Visiting Zelda's parents in Montgomery in early 1927 and his own parents at their new home in Washington, D.C., Scott must have seemed a much older man than the one they had last seen only three years earlier.

He was also poorer, in need of some fast cash, and sus-

Disillusioned by their experience in Europe, Scott and Zelda, with daughter Scottie, returned to the States in 1926.

ceptible to the overtures of Hollywood studios willing to pay high salaries to scriptwriters. Two weeks after he returned to the United States, he received an offer from Feature Productions, a production company working with United Artists. Feature Productions asked Scott to write a "fine modern college story" as a vehicle for the popular actress Constance Talmadge.[10]

Offered $3,500 as an enticement, and promised $12,500 upon acceptance of his script, Scott could not refuse. Leaving Scottie with his parents, he and Zelda set out for the West Coast in early January. They settled at the Ambassador Hotel in Los Angeles and attended parties with Hollywood's biggest stars, including Douglas Fairbanks and Mary Pickford, John Barrymore, movie executive Irving Thalberg—Scott's model for Monroe Stahr, the hero of his last novel, *The Last Tycoon*—and Lois Moran, a beautiful, flirtatious seventeen-year-old actress who would become the model for Scott's next fictional heroine, Rosemary Hoyt, in *Tender Is the Night*. But Hollywood did not offer as wide a variety of entertainments as New York or Paris; for the most part, it was a dull town where movie stars hid from the public gaze. Only occasionally, at night, did the city come alive. On those occasions, the Fitzgeralds tried to shine with their old brilliance. But their attention-grabbing pranks had grown stale by 1927. At one party, they borrowed the guests' jewels and boiled them in a pot of tomato soup. They arrived at another, a costume party given by studio chief Samuel Goldwyn, wearing pajamas instead of costumes. To gain admission, they crawled around the entrance, barked, and claimed to be dogs. These gags failed to convince Hollywood society of the Fitzgeralds' wit and charm, and Scott's screenplay for the Constance Talmadge movie, *Lipstick*, failed to convince the studios that he could translate his obvious skill as a fiction writer into a successful screenwriting career. Scott and Zelda returned to the East Coast in March. Denied the $12,500 payment for his awful screenplay, Scott had not improved his financial situation in Hollywood, nor had he boosted his social standing. Worst of all, Zelda harbored a grudge over Scott's obvious infatuation with Lois Moran.

With significantly limited resources, the Fitzgeralds searched the eastern seaboard for a new residence. In April, they found a three-story, thirty-room mansion called Ellerslie in Edgemoor, Delaware, along the banks of the Delaware River. Scott signed a three-year lease for $150 a month, a shockingly low sum. The rooms at Ellerslie were so large that

The Ellerslie mansion provided a spacious, cost-effective setting for the Fitzgeralds' party lifestyle.

Zelda designed oversized furniture for them. The mansion became, in effect, the Fitzgeralds' fantastic playhouse. They hosted raucous parties and invited all their friends—Lois Moran, Ernest Hemingway, Bunny Wilson, John Dos Passos, novelist/photographer Carl Van Vechten, playwright Thorton Wilder—for extended visits. Dos Passos later remembered nights when the Fitzgeralds provided their guests with too much alcohol but no food; others remembered how Scott would convince his butler to hide behind doors and groan like a ghost when his guests passed through the house.[11] When Scott was drunk, he alienated many of his closest friends; but he usually managed to repair his relationships when he sobered up. Only Zelda remained beyond his reach. Their arguments were beginning to turn violent as Scott, unhinged by drink, threw household objects or, on occasion, slapped her. When he lost control in public, he was often taken into police custody. In one of the most humiliating moments of this difficult period, he panicked before delivering a formal address at the Princeton Cottage Club (during his first visit back to campus since his official banishment seven years earlier), drank too much, and cut short his address by saying, simply, "God, I'm a lousy speaker!"[12] Meanwhile, Zelda retreated into a series of creative endeavors. She wrote articles for *Harper's Bazaar* and *College Humor*—and published a few sketches under Scott's name in order to earn higher fees—renewed her interest in painting and, finally, enrolled in ballet classes with Catherine Littlefield, director of the Philadelphia Opera Ballet Corps.

Between April 1927 and April 1928, Scott completed some important work on his novel, produced a few magazine items, and began writing a series of short stories that followed the life of a new alter ego, Basil Duke Lee. In the next year, he would write seven Basil stories, revisiting the people and events of his youth. But while he lingered on his past in his writing, he could not escape his present woes. His wife had entirely devoted herself to the ballet, in the hope of joining a professional troupe (though Zelda was too old, at twenty-seven, to merit serious consideration). His major novel was already years late. And he had run up a significant debt to Harold Ober to pay for his expenses at Ellerslie. Once again, the Fitzgeralds returned to Paris, where they stayed for five desperate months as they struggled to make sense of their predicament.

In Paris, Zelda took dance lessons from Lubov Egorova, a former head of the Diaghilev ballet school, and wife of the Russian noble Prince Trubetskoy. She surrendered herself to Egorova and pushed her body to its limits, practicing several times a day with manic energy. A few companies offered Zelda secondary roles—and several offended her by asking her to perform as a bawdy shimmy dancer—but she was determined to earn a place in one of the great Russian troupes. As she drifted deeper into her own obsessions, Scott tried to renew his ties to the expatriate community. He saw John Peale Bishop, humbled himself before James Joyce (who declared about his young admirer, "I think he must be mad. . . . He'll do himself injury some day."[13]) and encouraged the career of André Chamson, a young French novelist who soon became a Scribner's writer. But, unable to focus on his own work, he eventually succumbed to his alcoholism; he was arrested in July and again in August, ostensibly for public drunkenness.

After five months in Paris, the Fitzgeralds returned to Ellerslie in October 1928. There, Zelda continued her ballet lessons and earned the money to pay for them by selling a series of articles to *College Humor*. Scott, on the other hand, ignored his work and shared several drunken escapades with Philippe, a Parisian taxi driver whom he hired as a personal valet. Falling into a now-familiar pattern, he spent several nights at the local jail. When the lease to Ellerslie expired in March 1929, he and Zelda decided to try Europe yet again. As always, they hoped the change of scenery would inspire a change in their lives. They sailed to Genoa, visited the Riviera, stayed in Paris, and, during the summer, rented a villa in Cannes. Scott wrote a few new stories during the year—including a few more chapters for his novel—but he had not produced anything of real value in a long time. And now, as his alcoholism nearly erased his personal charm, he was beginning to scare away his friends. Hemingway was one of the first to withdraw. He had already refused to give Scott his new address in Paris, in fear that Scott would interrupt him when he was trying to work. But then came the now-legendary boxing match between Hemingway and writer Morely Callaghan, in which Scott served as timekeeper. When Scott absentmindedly allowed a round to continue longer than the agreed-upon time, and Callaghan knocked Hemingway to the floor, Hemingway berated Scott and stormed out of the gym. This seemingly insignificant incident haunted Scott, who tried to repair their friendship, and marked a turning point in Scott's relationship to his hero. By the spring of 1930, he would have to get his news about Hemingway from Max Perkins.[14]

On the heels of such disasters, Scott and Zelda tried one more move: In February 1930, they vacationed in Algiers on the North African coast. Scott hoped the trip would soothe Zelda's nerves. She had developed several disturbing tics during the most recent stay in Europe, laughing and muttering to herself and, on several occasions, endangering her life and the lives of the people around her. For a short time, it appeared that the Algerian excursion succeeded where previous vacations had failed; Scott and Zelda spent a relaxing month together. But she resumed her punishing dancing regimen as soon as they returned to Paris. At the end of April, she reached her physical and psychological limits simultaneously: She suffered her first breakdown.

A few months earlier, on October 24, 1929, a day known as Black Thursday, the American stock market crashed. After a decade of rampant optimism and irresponsible speculation, the world economy failed. The United States, having reveled in the Jazz Age that Scott Fitzgerald helped to create and celebrate, now faced the longest financial depression in its history. Millions of people lost their jobs; hunger became a fact of life for an increasing portion of the nation's population. The era of flappers and philosophers, of all-night parties in luxurious mansions, was over.

And just as the Jazz Age ended, Scott and Zelda, the glamorous couple that symbolized that giddy era, nearly lost everything.

Chapter 7

CRACK-UP

The marks of suffering are more comparable to the loss
of a finger, or of the sight of an eye. We do not miss
them, either, for one minute in a year, but if we should
there is nothing to be done about it.
                              —From *Tender Is the Night*[1]

Zelda entered Malmaison, a hospital outside Paris, on April
23, 1930. She stayed for a little more than a week, continu-
ally protesting her confinement and proclaiming her will to
dance: "It's dreadful, it's horrible, what's to become of me, I
must work and I won't be able to, I should die, but I must
work."[2] Ignoring her doctor's objections, she left the hospital
on May 2 and returned to the Fitzgeralds' Paris apartment,
where she continued her obsessive ballet training. Her condition deteriorated as Scott looked on helplessly. She started
hearing voices and hallucinating, and once again attempted
suicide. On May 22, she entered a second clinic, Valmont, in
Switzerland. The doctors at Valmont decided that she was too
sick for a simple rest cure. They called in a specialist, Dr. Oscar
Forel from Les Rives de Prangins, a high-ranking psychiatric
institute near Geneva. Before Zelda left Valmont with Dr.
Forel, the Valmont doctors filed a dire report describing her
condition:

> It was evident that the relationship between the patient
> and her husband had been weakened for a long time

and that for that reason the patient had not only attempted to establish her own life by the ballet (since the family life and her duties as a mother were not sufficient to satisfy her ambition and her artistic interest) but that she also [had withdrawn] from her husband. As far as her 8 year old daughter is concerned she expressed herself as follows to the question: "What role did her child play in her life?": "That is done now, I want to do something else."[3]

Observing Zelda's retreat from family life and her consuming passion for the ballet, Dr. Forel diagnosed her with schizophrenia and arranged for a long period of treatment.

As part of Zelda's cure, Dr. Forel asked Scott to stop drinking. But the writer refused. "Give up strong drink permanently I will," Scott wrote in reply. "Bind myself to forswear wine forever I cannot . . . I have lived hard and ruined the essential innocence in myself that could make it that possible, *and the fact that I have abused liquor* is something *to be paid for with suffering and death perhaps but not with renunciation.*"[4] Scott feared that by giving up alcohol he would be admitting his own responsibility for Zelda's collapse. Hurt by her most recent suggestions that he was the source of her problems, he could not allow her to blame him for her sickness. "We ruined ourselves," he concluded in one of the long, retrospective letters he wrote to her during her stay at Prangins. "I have never honestly thought that we ruined each other."[5]

While Scott bickered with her doctors about limiting his alcohol consumption, Zelda developed a painful eczema all over her body, a result of her intense psychological stress. Her moods changed rapidly. She accepted that she would never return to ballet, but she also tried to run away from Prangins and had to be confined for a short time. In a series of agonizing letters written during the summer of 1930, she apologized to Scott for the trouble she had caused him, and tried to explain her actions:

Try to understand that people are not always reasonable when the world is as unstable and vacillating as a sick head can render it—That for months I have been living in vaporous places peopled with one-dimensional figures and tremulous buildings until I can no longer tell an optical illusion from a reality—that head and ears incessantly throb and roads disappear, until finally I lost all control and powers of judgment and was semi-imbecilic when I arrived here.[6]

But every time her doctors thought Zelda could handle and even profit from a meeting with Scott, she would display some kind of manic behavior.

Scott spent the rest of 1930 shuttling between Prangins and Paris, where Scottie lived with a governess and attended school. Despite his own tenuous grip on reality, he tried to fulfill his responsibilities as a father and writer as well as a husband. During this period, his contacts with the outside world were brief and hurried. He spent two days with Thomas Wolfe, another young Scribner's writer whose 1929 novel, *Look Homeward, Angel*, received tremendous critical attention. He commiserated with Gerald Murphy, whose son Patrick was hospitalized in Switzerland with tuberculosis. And he embarked on the usual drinking sprees. Still, he managed to complete several short stories, including "One Trip Abroad," a tale of a couple's mental and moral disintegration that ends on the shores of Lake Geneva. He may not have produced anything else of real quality, but "One Trip Abroad" partially redeemed his summer. It became a trial run for the novel Scott had been trying to write for years. In its focus on psychological collapse, it suggested the path Scott finally took to complete *Tender Is the Night*. Perhaps it revived in him a more general interest in writing as well; in December, he wrote "Babylon Revisited," which would appear in the *Saturday Evening Post* in February 1931. Perhaps his greatest short story, "Babylon Revisited" explores the relationship between Charlie Wales, a lonely expatriate in Paris, and his daughter Honoraria, and reflects Scott's feelings for Scottie in the months following Zelda's breakdown.

At the beginning of 1931, Scott received sad news from Washington, D.C.: Edward Fitzgerald had died suddenly of a heart attack. He sailed home on the liner *New York* and arrived in Rockville, Maryland, in time for the funeral. Remembering a man who exhibited many of his own characteristics—alcoholism, weakness of will, good intentions—Scott complimented his father in his personal writings from this period: "I loved my father—always deep in my subconscious I have referred judgment back to him, what he would have thought, or done. He loved me—and felt a deep responsibility for me. . . ."[7] Scott seemed, at least for the moment, to have forgotten the embarrassment his family had once inspired in him.

While he was still in the States, he also visited the Sayres. Despite a history of mental illness in their own family, he knew that Zelda's sister Rosalind and her parents blamed him for Zelda's condition. Mrs. Sayre tried to maintain some civility during the reunion, but Judge Sayre—bedridden with his own illnesses—dismissed him. However, Zelda drew closer to him as she recovered. "Wasn't it fun to laugh together over the 'phone?" she wrote to him in 1931. "You are so infinitely sweet and dear—O my dear—my love, my infinitely inexpressible sweet darling dear, I love you so much."[8] To her doctors, she appeared well enough in July to accompany Scott and Scottie on a trip across the border into France, and then to join Scott and the Murphys in Germany in August. Encouraged by the ease with which Zelda faced these challenges, Dr. Forel signed her release from Prangins on September 15, 1931.

The Fitzgeralds were relieved to escape the sad pattern of the previous two years. Zelda's illness had stripped away her physical beauty; her face was haggard, her skin drew tighter on her face, and she had aged dramatically. But she seemed happier and more stable than she had been in years. To facilitate her recovery, the Fitzgeralds settled in a rented house in Cloverdale, Alabama, a suburb of Montgomery. Zelda worked at re-creating the family's home life while Scott tried to write his way out of debt. On top of the lingering bills from their old extravagances, Scott now had to pay for Zelda's treatment. Even the seventeen stories he wrote between 1930 and 1931 did not earn him enough to settle his accounts.

So in November 1931, he once again answered Hollywood's call. This time, Irving Thalberg, the famous producer and cocreator of Metro-Goldwyn-Mayer studios, asked him to work on a screenplay for a comedy called *Red-Headed Woman* and offered him a $1,200 weekly salary. Like his previous forays into the movie business, this five-week stint ended in disaster. Scott humiliated himself at a party at Thalberg's mansion, insulting guests and forcing everyone to listen to his rendition of "Dog! Dog! Dog!," a silly tune he wrote in college. He would soon transform the entire episode into "Crazy Sunday," one of his best short stories from this period, but it did not bode well for his screenwriting career. Thalberg ultimately rejected his script for *Red-Headed Woman*, paid him $6,000, and fired him before Christmas.

Meanwhile, Zelda remained in Cloverdale, planning a novel of her own, writing short stories (one of which, "Miss Ella," appeared in *Scribner's Magazine*), and caring for her father, who was still suffering from flu complications. Judge Sayre died on November 19, while Scott was still in Hollywood. In mourning, Zelda developed many of her old symptoms: eczema, insomnia, and asthma. She suffered bouts of hysteria, and the crises became more and more frequent. By mid-February, the Fitzgeralds no longer had any choice; they drove to Baltimore, and Zelda entered the Henry Phipps Psychiatric Clinic of the Johns Hopkins University Hospital.

Despite severe hardships, Zelda's second stay at a psychiatric institution was one of the most productive periods of her life. During her first month at Phipps, she completed her novel, *Save Me the Waltz*, and sent it directly to Max Perkins. To Scott, who had been working on his own novel for almost seven years, the sheer speed with which Zelda wrote was humiliating. But when he finally read her manuscript he noticed that she lifted entire episodes from his unpublished work. Worse still, she named the book's male protagonist—a critical depiction of Scott—Amory Blaine, the name of the main character in *This Side of Paradise*. Professional jealousy aside, Scott knew that his family's future depended on the success of his own novel, since his reputation sold books and earned higher pay rates. Anything Zelda did to jeopardize the sales of *Tender Is the Night*, whenever it would be published, endangered not only his career as a writer but also the family's financial security. He wrote a series of angry letters to Zelda's doctors, begging them to intercede on his behalf and delay the publication of her novel. And then he wrote to Perkins: "My God, my books made her a legend and her single intention in this somewhat thin portrait is to make me a non-entity. That's why she sent the book directly to New York."[9]

Two weeks after this crisis, however, Scott wired Max that Scribner's could publish a revised version of *Save Me the Waltz*; Scott and Zelda edited the manuscript together, improved it in places, tempered her obvious attacks on Scott's character, and changed the male protagonist's name to David Knight. The finished product, a biography of Zelda's alter ego, Alabama Knight, includes depictions of several episodes from the Fitzgeralds' lives that Scott would also explore in his own novel, including Zelda's affair with Josanne. Still, their books were very different. Zelda saw things through a fantastic lens and wrote with a freer hand than her husband. She described David Knight's personality, for instance, as a thing that opens and closes "like the tentacles of a carnivorous maritime plant"; and she gave Alabama the "live eyes of a soft wild animal" that peer out "in skeptic invitation from the taut net of her features."[10] The dreamlike quality of Zelda's language suggested that she had real potential as a writer, and had developed a voice that differed from her husband's tight, musical style. But *Save Me the Waltz* was an uneven book, an immature first effort. Scribner's published it in October 1932 to mediocre reviews. It sold fewer than 1,400 copies and earned Zelda $120 in royalties. Only the Fitzgeralds' marriage seemed affected by its publication: *Save Me the Waltz* introduced new resentments into their already troubled relationship.

After her second breakdown, Scott began to accept Zelda's sickness as a permanent condition. He came to expect that the next few years of her life would follow a pattern of collapse and recovery. So in May he rented an enormous Victorian house called La Paix ("The Peace") close to the Phipps Clinic in Rodgers Forge, north of Baltimore. The house was owned by an architect, Bayard Turnbull, whose cultured wife,

This photograph of the Fitzgeralds, out on the town in 1932, shows the strain both had endured over the years.

Margaret, was a friend of the poet T. S. Eliot and an admirer of Scott's. (In later years, the Turnbull's son, Andrew, became Scott's biographer.) At the end of June 1932, Zelda's doctors released her from the clinic and Scottie returned from one of her long separations from her parents. The reunited Fitzgeralds attempted to restore a sense of normality to their lives. As inexperienced parents, Scott and Zelda tried to protect Scottie and prevent her from repeating their own mistakes by criticizing her harshly and nagging her constantly. Luckily for Scottie, they spent most of their days working. Zelda continued to write and paint while Scott, with the help of a secretary, Isabel Owens, completed his book.

What Scott had first planned in 1925 as a story about a man's catastrophic relationship with his mother had evolved by 1932 into a novel about the collapse of a marriage. *Tender Is the Night* follows the lives of a successful psychologist, Dick Diver, and his wife and former patient Nicole. Blending the characteristics of the Murphys and the Fitzgeralds, the Divers appear to their friends as an ideal couple: Dick, who "seemed kind and charming" with a voice that promised to "unroll an endless succession of magnificent possibilities," and Nicole, with a face that "had been made first on the heroic scale with strong structure and marking."[11] They host parties on the French Riviera, support important artists and writers—including Abe North, a representation of Ring Lardner—and seem happy with their lives. But, unbeknownst to their friends, they have become dangerously dependent on each other, "one and equal, not apposite and complementary."[12] For this reason, a change in one necessitates an equal but opposite change in the other: As Nicole recovers from her schizophrenia, Dick declines. When he begins an affair with a beautiful, young actress, Rosemary Hoyt (based on Lois Moran), she pursues her own affair with a handsome mercenary, Tommy Barban (a composite of Edouard Josanne and Tommy Hickock, the polo star who also served as the model for Tom Buchanan in *The Great Gatsby*). In this battle of wills, Nicole proves to be the stronger of the two; she chooses Barban as Dick seeks comfort in alcohol. In their climactic confrontation, Nicole completes the reversal of their relationship: "For almost the first time in her life she was sorry for him—it is hard for those who have once been mentally afflicted to be sorry for those who are well . . . That he no longer controlled her—did he know that?"[13] When Dick finally realizes how little he means to her, he leaves Europe and retreats to an anonymous, insignificant psychiatric practice in upstate New York.

At La Paix, Scott settled into a steady writing routine that was both productive and therapeutic. Perhaps he even gained new insights into his marriage as he completed *Tender Is the Night*. But Zelda's disease changed constantly as she exhibited new, dangerous symptoms. In June 1933, she tried to burn old clothes in the house's second-story fireplace, but set fire to the roof instead. The local press photographed the author and his wife on their front lawn after the fire, with their salvaged possessions scattered around them. Scott felt he could not spare any more time away from his novel, so he delayed house repairs until after he finished his book, and wrote the final chapters in rooms that were sooty, water damaged, and dreary.

A week after the fire, a Baltimore theater troupe—the Junior Vagabonds—performed *Scandalabra*, the play Zelda had written during the previous year. Despite Scott's determined efforts to shape her sprawling, five-hour farce into a leaner production, *Scandalabra* flopped just as *The Vegetable* had ten years earlier; the audience walked out on opening night. After this disappointment, Zelda concentrated more of her attention on her expressive, hallucinatory paintings. A month later, she learned that her brother Anthony, suffering his own bout of depression, committed suicide in a hospital in Mobile, Alabama. This news, on the heels of the *Scandalabra* disaster, started Zelda on another downward spiral.

Meanwhile, Scott made several halfhearted attempts to control his drinking. He finally acknowledged that his dependence on gin was weakening him physically, hurting his family, and even undermining his writing. Magazines were rejecting his stories for the first time in his career. Yet he surrendered to alcohol once again in late 1933, when faced with a series of new crises. His income had declined so precipitously since 1931 that he had to borrow more money from Harold Ober. He learned in September that Ring Lardner died after his own long battle with alcoholism. And finally, after he finished his novel, and moved his family to a smaller house in downtown Baltimore, Zelda suffered her third breakdown.

On February 12, 1934, she reentered Phipps. A month later, Scott moved her to Craig House, a hospital in Beacon, New York. In May, she moved again, this time to Sheppard and Enoch Pratt Hospital in Towson, Maryland. Finally, two years later, she entered Highland Hospital in Asheville, North Carolina. All told, she would spend more than six years in mental health institutions after this third collapse.

Chapter 8

INTO THE SUNSET

> When I arrived, he quit and took the bottle and retired
> to a chair just out of the floodlight, watching in dark
> dangerous majest. He was pale—he was so transparent
> that you could almost watch the alcohol mingle with the
> poison of his exhaustion.
>
> —From *The Last Tycoon*[1]

As Scott negotiated Zelda's treatment, an abridged version of *Tender Is the Night* appeared in four installments in *Scribner's Magazine* under the title "Richard Diver, a Romance." Scott did not settle on the final title, a quotation from John Keats's "Ode to a Nightingale," until the book version was published on April 23, 1934. As expected for a book that had been written over eight years and under the most trying circumstances— Scott later claimed he had written Part III "entirely on stimulant"[2]—*Tender Is the Night* earned mixed reviews. But fiction writers generally celebrated Scott's return to form. Usually a harsh critic of Scott's life and work, John Peale Bishop offered some of the strongest praise: "You have shown us what we have waited so long and impatiently to see, that you are a true, a beautiful, a tragic poet."[3] John Dos Passos and Carl Van Vechten followed suit. Even the Murphys, to whom Scott dedicated the book, acknowledged its literary merit, though they objected to its unflattering depiction of their lives. (Sara Murphy had already criticized Scott earlier in the decade for his probing questions and tendency to treat his friends as literary subjects: "You can't expect anyone to like or stand a continual feeling of analysis and subanalysis and criticism . . . If you don't know what people are like it's your loss."[4] With the publication of *Tender Is the Night*, Scott proved her concerns were justified.) Only Hemingway disappointed him. Papa remained silent, despite Scott's plea for his opinion. When he finally spoke up, he chastised Scott for creating composite characters in Dick and Nicole Diver, and distorting the Murphys' lives as well as his and Zelda's. Always spiteful toward other writers—and particularly those who helped him in the past—Hemingway only praised the novel in a letter to Max Perkins: "It's amazing how excellent much of it is. Much of it is better than anything else he ever wrote."[5]

Given the warm reception the novel received among his friends, Scott was bitterly disappointed to learn that it sold only thirteen thousand copies. He had staked Scottie's education, Zelda's treatment, and his own survival on *Tender Is the Night*, only to watch it become the biggest commercial failure of his career. As he had after the publication of his previous novels, Scott compiled a short story collection, *Taps at Reveille*, to follow *Tender Is the Night* into the bookstores. It included "Babylon Revisited" and "Crazy Sunday," a fictionalized account of Scott's experiences in Hollywood, but was dominated by the flimsy tales of Basil Duke Lee and Josephine, recounting his own experiences with Ginevra King. *Taps* flopped as well.

Ironically, just when Scott's boy-meets-girl magazine formula had run its course, Scott initiated a series of relationships with other women to compensate for Zelda's absence. Few lasted long, although some of the women, such as the writer Dorothy Parker, remained close to him for the rest of his life. He relied on his second secretary, Laura Guthrie Hearne, to help him sort through the various seductions and breakups. However, he could never bring himself to abandon his wife, to whom he was bound the way Dick Diver was bound to Nicole.

Through 1935, he shuttled between Baltimore and Asheville, North Carolina, where several of his friends resided. During one visit to Asheville in March, he visited a medical clinic and discovered that he was experiencing the early stages of tuberculosis. The disease had already damaged his lungs. Of course he ignored the doctors' warnings and continued to

Writer Dorothy Parker, 1932

drink and smoke to excess. But the knowledge that his health was poor, when added to his concerns for Zelda and Scottie, his inability to write, his rampant alcoholism, and his various romantic entanglements, weighed heavily on his mind.

In November, during an attempt to escape the complications of his life, he ran from his friends and landed at a cheap hotel in the small town of Hendersonville, North Carolina. Alone, debt ridden, distraught over his wife's sickness, his own sickness, and his professional failures, he nursed himself back to health after a harrowing experience he called a "crack-up"— a nervous breakdown. "Things rather crashed again," he wrote in a letter to Harold Ober.[6] Unable to concentrate on his fiction during his stay in Hendersonville, he turned his attention to his own sickness and recovery and composed three essays about his self-discoveries. These "Crack-Up" essays were the most serious, focused attempts Scott had ever made to dissect his own personality. His problem, he decided, was a kind of moral drift, the realization that he "would never be as good a man again."[7] In his drive for success, he had split his personality among friends such as Bunny Wilson, Hemingway, and Gerald Murphy; like an insecure college boy, he let them determine how he would live and write. "So there was not an 'I' any more," he concluded, "not a basis on which I could organize my self-respect."[8] In the final essay, he vows to become "a writer only": "The man I had persistently tried to be became such a burden that I have 'cut him loose.' "[9] For Scott Fitzgerald, a person who had spent his entire life trying to achieve fame, influence, and popularity, the "Crack-Up" essays suggested a true rebirth.

He returned to Baltimore to start the new year, sold the new essays to *Esquire* magazine (they appeared from February through April), and moved Zelda to Highland Hospital in Asheville. He hoped the Highland doctors' techniques, including a rigorous exercise schedule and a series of coma-inducing insulin injections, would have a better effect on her than her previous treatments. Soon, Zelda was writing letters from Highland that raised the possibility of her full recovery: "And maybe everything is going to be all right, after all. There are so many houses I'd like to live in with you. Oh Wont you be mine—again and again—and yet again—"[10] But both Scott and Zelda knew they were holding on to impossible dreams.

Soon after the "Crack-Up" essays appeared in *Esquire*, Scott found that his honest self-examinations had made him an object of public ridicule. Hemingway struck first, as he always did when he sensed weakness in a fellow writer. In the August 1936 edition of *Esquire*, he published "The Snows of Kilimanjaro," a story about a dying writer who regrets the way he had wasted his talent. Searching his memory for other writers who failed to live up to their potential, the story's main character remembers "poor Scott Fitzgerald," who thought that rich people "were a special glamorous race and when he found they weren't it wrecked him just as much as any other thing that wrecked him." Humiliated that his friend and hero could mock him publicly, Fitzgerald begged Max Perkins to remove his name from any reprintings of the story. (Hemingway later replaced "Scott Fitzgerald" with "Julian.") Then, in late September, the New York *Post* printed an interview called "The Other Side of Paradise," which depicted Scott as a weak, ineffectual drunk. Like Hemingway, the *Post*'s interviewer, Michel Mok, exploited Scott's confessions in the "Crack-Up" essays and savaged his reputation. These and similar depictions of "poor Scott Fitzgerald" dominated Scott's public image for the rest of his life.

In the month between Hemingway's and Mok's attacks, Mollie Fitzgerald died of a cerebral hemorrhage. Now parentless, Scott once again confronted his own mortality. But, after sorting through his mother's possessions, Scott wrote his sister Annabel a letter that, like the "Crack-Up" essays, displayed his new maturity as well as his new understanding of and tolerance for other people. Hemingway and Mok may have ridiculed him, but he was finally growing up:

> Mother and I never had anything in common except a relentless stubborn quality, but when I saw all this it turned me inside out realizing how unhappy her temperament made her and how she clung, to the end, to all things that would remind her of moments of snatched happiness. So I couldn't bear to throw out anything, even that rug, and it all goes to storage.[11]

Mollie had always embarrassed Scott, and he had distanced himself from her since his childhood. Now that he recognized the effects of his own weaknesses, however, he saw his mother differently. He realized that she was an unhappy person who struggled against her eccentricities, a person much like himself.

But none of these new understandings helped in his relationship with Scottie. By most accounts, Scottie was a typically

rebellious teenager who handled the facts of her childhood—
an alcoholic father, a schizophrenic mother, a dependence
upon a series of governesses—surprisingly well. Yet, out of love
for his daughter and concern that she follow a smoother course
through life, Scott became an intolerant parent. Even Scottie's
ordinary complaints about the difficulties of boarding school
life sparked his anger and drew harsh replies:

> Why are you whining about such matters as study hall,
> etc., when you deliberately picked this school as the
> place you wanted to go above all places? Of course it is

Fourteen-year-old Scottie found Fitzgerald a solicitous father
determined to spare her from the woes her parents suffered.

hard. Nothing any good isn't hard, and you know you have never been brought up soft, or are you quitting on me suddenly? Darling, you know I love you, and I expect you to live up absolutely to what I laid out for you in the beginning.[12]

To Scott's disappointment, his conflicts with Scottie only increased with time (and reached a climax when she was suspended from the Ethel Walker School in Connecticut in 1937 for leaving campus without permission). But he did not give up on her, just as he never gave up on Zelda. Despite his financial difficulties, he insisted that his daughter receive a top-rate education, and that his wife receive top-rate care.

By the middle of 1937, after receiving several more story rejections and watching his debt to Harold Ober increase dramatically, he decided to make a final sacrifice for his family. He returned to Hollywood, the site of so many past humiliations, and joined the screenwriting staff at Metro-Goldwyn-Mayer. MGM paid him $1,000 per week, which he then divided among Scottie, Zelda, Harold Ober, and Scribner's—by 1938, he would settle all his debts. He even stopped drinking, despite the intense social pressures he faced while living with the hard-drinking screenwriters at the Garden of Allah hotel on Sunset Boulevard. Most of the people who had known Scott for a long time and saw him again in Hollywood—Dorothy Parker, John O'Hara, Ring Lardner, Jr.—noticed a frightening change in him. The gray pallor of his face and his quiet humility shocked anyone who expected to meet the charming, dangerous, tireless hero of the Jazz Age.[13] He looked small and sickly. But he was determined to succeed. Instead of gin, Scott now drank several bottles of Coca-Cola a day and ate vast quantities of candy and sweets. He studied screenwriting and movie production with intense interest. And he found comfort in a new companion, Sheilah Graham.

Graham was the kind of person Scott wrote about, but not the kind of person he usually befriended. Born Lily Sheil in 1904, Graham was raised in the East End of London, orphaned when she was six years old, and seemed destined to live a life of poverty. Fortunately, she was beautiful and caught the attention

Gossip columnist Sheilah Graham had a volatile though
supportive relationship with Scott.

of an older businessman, Major John Graham Gillam, who
married her, encouraged her to change her name, and paid for
her acting lessons. She became a chorus girl, and then a fixture
of English high society. In 1933, she emigrated to the United
States and became a gossip columnist for the *New York Evening
Journal*. She divorced Gillam in 1937 and promised to marry

another gossip columnist by the end of the year. Instead, she fell in love with Scott. Her entire persona—her aristocratic manners and appearance—was as phony as Jay Gatsby's. But she remained faithful to Scott during his final, stormy days in Hollywood, and cared for him during the last years of his life.

Scott's initial work for MGM was as poor as his previous screenwriting attempts had been. Though a master of written dialogue, he did not know how to write dramatic dialogue. And he hated the way the studio treated its writers. To Scott, the creative process demanded more time and energy than studio executives allowed him. His greatest success, and his only screen credit, was his adaptation of Erich Remarque's anti-Nazi novel, *Three Comrades*. Against Scott's wishes, the movie's producer Joseph Mankiewicz assigned an old acquaintance, Ted Paramore, as his cowriter to the movie. Scott hated Paramore's changes, but hated Mankiewicz's changes even more. Worse still, Hollywood's movie censors decided that the movie's anti-Nazi themes would threaten U.S. foreign policy. Mankiewicz simply eliminated those themes from the final product. Scott's work on the movie earned him a contract for another year with MGM, but his *Three Comrades* experience spoiled his enthusiasm. He produced little of quality during the rest of his screenwriting days.

For the most part, Scott tried to remain sober through 1937, but he was fighting an uphill battle. His frequent visits to Zelda proved traumatic. His conflicts with Mankiewicz and the studio increased. And a surprise meeting with Ginevra King in October, the first such meeting in twenty-one years, unsettled him for weeks. Still reeling from that experience, he accompanied Sheilah Graham to Chicago, where she was scheduled to deliver a radio broadcast. The trip was a disaster. He started drinking on the plane, tried to punch the radio show's producer, and ended up in his hotel room with Harold Gingrich, the editor of *Esquire*, who sobered him up by force-feeding him food and coffee. After this episode, his binges became more frequent. When he was at his worst, he and Sheilah fought violently.

He worked on an original script for a film called *Infidelity* in January 1938. Like *Three Comrades*, it ran afoul of Hollywood's strict censors, who objected to its depiction of troubled marriages. As he waited to hear the censors' final verdict—a total rejection—he took Zelda and Scottie to Virginia Beach for a vacation. Sadly, his attempt to renew his family's love backfired: He drank incessantly, Zelda ranted incoherently, and they argued for days. When he returned to Hollywood, Sheilah checked him into a medical clinic for treatment of his tuberculosis. Recognizing that his health deteriorated with each drink, she moved him away from the writers' parties at the Garden of Allah. He rented a small house in Malibu, almost an hour away from the studios, and withdrew from Hollywood's social life. Nevertheless, he completed little work. In his extensive free time, he concentrated on Sheilah's education; at her request, he designed a vast curriculum much like the one he had put together for Scottie years earlier. In the fall, he moved again, this time to a house with cheaper rent in the San Fernando Valley. He needed to cut his expenses since MGM dropped his contract at the end of 1938.

Cut loose by the big studio, he was soon hired by producer David O. Selznick to adapt Margaret Mitchell's best-selling novel, *Gone with the Wind*, for the big screen. Fired from that project after two weeks, he signed on with Walter Wanger at United Artists to cowrite a screenplay about the Dartmouth College Winter Carnival. His partner was twenty-five-year-old Budd Schulberg, who later documented their experiences together in his novel, *The Disenchanted*. Wanger insisted that his writers actually visit the carnival in February 1939, ignoring the possibility that a return to college life would tempt both men away from their work. As a result, Scott drank incessantly, embarrassed Wanger before the Dartmouth faculty, and got himself and Schulberg fired. Once again, Sheilah checked him into a hospital to help him recover from his binge. He had given up on sobriety altogether.

The Dartmouth fiasco effectively ruined his reputation in Hollywood. Few producers would hire him after Wanger spread the story of his dissipation. Holed up in Malibu, he devoted what little strength and energy he had left to his fiction and his drinking. He hired a recent college graduate, Frances

Kroll, as his secretary and began work on a novel about the movie business. He also wrote twenty-four short stories during this last active period, including seventeen about a Hollywood screenwriter named Pat Hobby, who can never find work.

He interrupted his writing in April to attempt one final spree with Zelda. He picked her up in Asheville and they flew to Havana, Cuba. Like the Virginia Beach vacation, this trip only underscored their estrangement. Zelda lost herself in a new religious fervor while Scott picked a fight with a cab-driver and was pummeled by an angry mob after he tried to break up a cockfight. From Cuba, they flew to New York, where Zelda left him to seek further medical treatment for his tuberculosis. On her own, she returned to Highland Hospital. They never saw each other again.

Scott spent two months in bed after the Cuba trip, writing when he could. Sad and frustrated, he fought bitterly with Sheilah. During a particularly bad stretch, she stayed away from him for five weeks. At the same time, he broke off relations with his loyal agent, Harold Ober. For years, Ober had been lending Scott money while the writer tried to produce his next salable item. Ober also served as Scottie's surrogate father while Scott and Zelda struggled with their physical and psychological problems. But in July 1939, Ober decided that he could not save Scott from another financial crisis. Ober knew that most of Scott's novels were out of print, and that he could no longer sell enough short stories to pay his debts. Scott had always been an expensive friend, but now he was a liability. Distressed about Ober's decision, Scott turned to Max Perkins and Gerald Murphy for support and put more pressure on himself to succeed with his new novel. Luckily, he sold the movie rights to "Babylon Revisited." The proceeds from this sale sustained him through much of 1940.

He moved back to Hollywood, into an apartment around the corner from Schwab's drugstore, a famous movie industry hangout. Surviving on liquor, sleeping pills, and heart medicine, he wrote a third of the novel Bunny Wilson would later edit and publish under the title *The Last Tycoon*. When it appeared in 1941, after Scott's death, a host of critics called it one of his

Van Johnson and Elizabeth Taylor starred in MGM's 1954
film *The Last Time I Saw Paris*, an adaptation of
"Babylon Revisited."

best works, perhaps even better than *The Great Gatsby*.[14] As
Scott intended, it revived his reputation as a major American
writer. Tragically, he was not around to enjoy his success.

The Last Tycoon is the story of Monroe Stahr, a producer
who, like Irving Thalberg of MGM, rose from humble origins
to become one of the most powerful men in Hollywood.
Through the eyes of the book's young narrator, Celia Brady,
the daughter of studio head Pat Brady, Stahr is a genius, a man
who has discovered "a new way of measuring our jerky hopes and
graceful rogueries and awkward sorrows" and has translated his
vision into popular movies.[15] He is masterful in his dealings
with executives, writers, cameramen, and actors, and has the
best creative instincts in the city. Better yet, he is a true leader,
a foil for Jay Gatsby and Dick Diver, a dreamer who actually
realizes his dreams. At the beginning of the novel, Stahr learns

that he is dying of a heart ailment and seeks a final romance with a British woman, Kathleen Moore, who reminds him of his dead wife. Before long, he is spending more time with Kathleen than with his studio employees, and he begins to lose the commanding presence he had displayed in the early chapters. Scott's outlines for the remaining portions of the novel, which Wilson published along with the written text, suggest that Stahr and Brady ultimately struggle for control of the studio, with Brady using Kathleen as a pawn in his power play.

The brilliance of the existing chapters and the remaining outline of *The Last Tycoon* prompted writers, critics, and readers to rediscover Scott's other works in the years following his death. But the six thousand words Scott sent to *Collier's* in November 1939 did not convince the magazine's editor, Kenneth Littauer, to buy the serial rights as he had promised. So Scott labored on in secrecy, without encouragement, until late November 1940. Then, weak from the exertion of writing a novel, and from his various illnesses, he collapsed in Schwab's drugstore. Doctors told him he had suffered a heart attack. No longer able to climb three flights of stairs to his own apartment, he moved into Sheilah's first-floor apartment nearby. On December 6, he wrote to Zelda, who had been released from Highland and was living in Montgomery with her mother, "Everything is my novel now—it has become of absorbing interest."[16] A week later, he wrote his last, fatherly warning to Scottie: "You have got two beautiful bad examples of parents. Just do everything we didn't do and you will be perfectly safe." But before closing his letter, he wrote a few more lines in defense of the woman who shared with him his greatest successes and his worst failures. "Be sweet to your mother," he told Scottie. "The insane are always mere guests on earth, eternal strangers carrying around broken decalogues that they cannot read."[17]

On December 20, he finished the first episode in chapter 6 of *The Last Tycoon* and asked Sheilah to postpone his doctor's visit so that they could celebrate. They went to the movies, but Scott complained of weakness, and perhaps a second heart attack, on the way home. Expecting to see a doctor the following day, he went to sleep that night. The next morning, he seemed better. He read the newspaper and, while waiting for his doctor to arrive, scanned an article about the Princeton football team in his alumni magazine. Suddenly, he toppled to the floor. It was his third heart attack in less than a month. By the time Sheilah could find help, forty-four-year-old F. Scott Fitzgerald was dead.

In his original will, Scott had requested that his estate "provide for a funeral and burial in keeping with my station in life." In the year before his death, he changed the provision; as a poor, forgotten writer, he wanted "the cheapest funeral," one "without undue ostentation or unnecessary expense."[18] He wished to be buried near his parents in St. Mary's Catholic Cemetery in Rockville, Maryland, but the local bishop refused to bury a lapsed Catholic in consecrated ground. On December 27, his body was interred at Rockville Union Cemetery. Zelda was too upset to attend the funeral.

In 1975, a different bishop decided to grant Scott's wish after a thirty-five-year delay: He moved the bodies of Scott and Zelda Fitzgerald to St. Mary's and buried them beneath a gravestone etched with the last line from *The Great Gatsby*: "So we beat on, boats against the current, borne back ceaselessly into the past."[19]

Between Scott's death in 1940 and her own in 1948, Zelda returned to Highland Hospital three times. During her last stay, she was trapped in a fire on the top floor of the hospital's central building. Zelda and eight other women died in the blaze.

Scottie graduated from Vassar College in 1944 and worked as a journalist for a variety of publications including *The New Yorker*, *Time*, *The Washington Post*, and the *New York Times*. She married a naval officer, Samuel Jackson Lanahan, in 1943, and raised four children. She later divorced Lanahan and married a man named Grove Smith, whom she divorced in 1980. Scottie died in 1986.

EPILOGUE

I write to you from the depths of one of my unholy
depressions. The book is wonderful—I honestly think
that when its published I shall be the best American novelist (which isn't saying a lot) but the end seems far away.
 —From a letter to Max Perkins, December 27, 1925[1]

F. Scott Fitzgerald's life followed the arc of a standard tragedy.
He rose from obscurity to the height of his profession. But
the very qualities that made him a success—his innocence,
his restlessness, his incessant dreaming, his sense of indestruc-
tibility—also contributed to his downfall.

In *This Side of Paradise*, he described the new freedoms he
saw sweeping through American society in the 1920s, and the
reading public responded to his vision with great enthusiasm.
But the carefree, glamorous lifestyle that he and Zelda embodied exacted a high price. They could not keep the party going
forever. Like a number of other twentieth-century icons—
Elvis Presley, James Dean, Marilyn Monroe, Jimi Hendrix,
Kurt Cobain—Scott and Zelda Fitzgerald lived hard and died
young.

At least, that is the Fitzgerald legend.

But the legend is deceiving. In reality, Scott and Zelda
fought hard to survive. In spite of his alcoholism and her
schizophrenia, they never surrendered to their difficulties. In
the "Crack-Up" essays, Scott left a record of his heroic struggle to understand and improve his life. In his letters to Scottie,

At forty, Scott's alcoholism and depression had
noticeably aged him.

he left a record of his fatherly love. And he died as he was writing the novel that would restore his reputation. Like Scott,
Zelda left her own letters, stories, and paintings as evidence of
her struggles. When she died at Highland Hospital in 1948,
she was trying to get well.

More important than the legend, then, is the work. After
Scott died, Edmund "Bunny" Wilson initiated a renaissance in
Fitzgerald studies. He edited and published *The Last Tycoon* in
1941 and *The Crack-Up*, a collection of Scott's essays, letters,
and notebook entries, in 1945. Also in 1945, Dorothy Parker
edited *The Portable Fitzgerald*, which introduced his work to
new generations of Americans. Since then, Scott and Zelda

Robert Redford and Mia Farrow in the 1974 version of *The Great Gatsby*; Jack Nicholson, Robert De Niro, and Theresa Russell in *The Last Tycoon,* 1976

have been the subjects of countless essays, articles, and biographies. Movie studios have adapted dozens of his stories to the big screen, including a 1974 version of *The Great Gatsby*, starring Robert Redford and Mia Farrow, and a 1976 version of *The Last Tycoon*, starring Robert De Niro. And scholars continue to unearth and publish new letter collections and manuscripts from Fitzgerald's extensive files.

These collections, films, and discoveries have kept Fitzgerald in the newspapers ever since his death. But, ultimately, he alone is responsible for his lasting popularity in the United States and across the world. In "May Day," "Absolution," "Babylon Revisited," and "Crazy Sunday," he created some of the finest short fiction ever written. And with *This Side of Paradise, Tender Is the Night, The Last Tycoon*, and especially *The Great Gatsby*—the ultimate meditation on the American Dream—he proved himself one of the most unique, astute, and important writers in American literature.

"You can take your hats off now, gentleman, and I think perhaps you had better," wrote the poet Stephen Vincent Benét when summing up Fitzgerald's career in 1941. "This is not a legend, this is a reputation—and, seen in perspective, it may well be one of the most secure reputations of our time."[2]

FOR FURTHER INFORMATION

BIOGRAPHIES

Bruccoli, Matthew J. *Fitzgerald and Hemingway: A Dangerous Friendship*. New York: Carroll & Graf Publishers, 1994.

Le Vot, André. *F. Scott Fitzgerald: A Biography*. New York: Warner Books, 1983.

Mellow, James R. *Invented Lives: F. Scott and Zelda Fitzgerald*. Boston: Houghton Mifflin Company, 1984.

Meyers, Jeffrey. *Scott Fitzgerald*. New York: Cooper Square Press, 1994.

Milford, Nancy. *Zelda: A Biography*. New York: Harper & Row, 1970.

LETTERS AND ESSAYS

Fitzgerald, F. Scott. *A Life in Letters*. New York: Touchstone, 1994.

———. *The Crack Up*. ed. Edmund Wilson. New York: New Directions, 1993.

Fitzgerald, Zelda. *The Collected Writings of Zelda Fitzgerald*. Tuscaloosa: The University of Alabama Press, 1991. (Includes Zelda's essays and stories, complete versions of her novels and plays, and several of her letters to her husband.)

Hemingway, Ernest. *A Moveable Feast*. New York: Scribner's, 1987. (Hemingway's account of life among the American expatriates in Paris.)

FICTION BY F. SCOTT FITZGERALD

Scribner's has reprinted all of Fitzgerald's fiction in paperback editions. Included here are the works Fitzgerald published—or intended to publish—in his own lifetime. Several manuscripts and unpublished works have appeared since his death.

This Side of Paradise, 1920
The Beautiful and Damned, 1922
The Vegetable, or, From President to Postman, 1923 (a play)
The Great Gatsby, 1925
Tender Is the Night, 1934
The Last Tycoon, 1941 (unfinished)
The Short Stories of F. Scott Fitzgerald, ed. Matthew J. Bruccoli, 1989
    (This survey of Fitzgerald's short stories includes forty-three
    stories, with the editor's helpful introductions to each. Scrib-
    ner's has also published several other, less complete collections.)

FITZGERALD MOVIES

This list includes only films and adaptations produced by major Hollywood studios.

The Chorus Girl's Romance, Metro, 1920 (adaptation of "Head and
    Shoulders")
The Off-Shore Pirate, Metro, 1921
The Beautiful and Damned, Warner Bros., 1922
Grit, Film Guild, 1924
The Great Gatsby, Famous Players/Paramount,1926
Three Comrades, MGM, 1938 (Fitzgerald cowrote the screenplay)
The Great Gatsby, Paramount, 1949
The Last Time I Saw Paris, MGM, 1954 (adaptation of "Babylon
    Revisited")
Tender Is the Night, 20th Century Fox, 1961
The Great Gatsby, Paramount, 1974
The Last Tycoon, Paramount, 1976

WEB SITE

University of South Carolina F. Scott Fitzgerald Centenary:
    http://www.sc.edu/fitzgerald/

NOTES

INTRODUCTION

[1] F. Scott Fitzgerald, *The Beautiful and Damned* (New York, 1995): 73.
[2] Andre Le Vot, *F. Scott Fitzgerald: A Biography* (New York, 1983): 85; Jeffrey Meyers, *Scott Fitzgerald: A Biography* (New York, 1994): 69; James R. Mellow, *Invented Lives: F. Scott and Zelda Fitzgerald* (Boston, 1984): 95.
[3] F. Scott Fitzgerald, *The Crack-Up*, ed. Edmund Wilson (New York, 1993): 90.

CHAPTER 1

[1] F. Scott Fitzgerald, *This Side of Paradise* (New York, 1996): 28–9.
[2] Le Vot: 5.
[3] Meyers: 5.
[4] Ibid: 4.
[5] Ibid: 7.
[6] F. Scott Fitzgerald, *A Life in Letters*, ed. Matthew J. Bruccoli (New York, 1994): 5.
[7] Arthur Mizener, *F. Scott Fitzgerald* (New York, 1972): 13.
[8] Meyers: 12–13.
[9] Quoted in Meyers: 15.

CHAPTER 2

[1] *This Side of Paradise*: 49.
[2] Ibid: 33.

[3] Le Vot: 30.
[4] Ibid: 41.
[5] Quoted in Meyers: 22.
[6] *A Life in Letters:* 8.
[7] Ibid: 8.
[8] Mizener: 28.
[9] Le Vot: 47.
[10] Meyers: 32.
[11] *The Crack-Up:* 76.
[12] *A Life in Letters:* 12.
[13] Ibid: 14.

CHAPTER 3

[1] F. Scott Fitzgerald, *The Great Gatsby* (New York, 1925): 76.
[2] Meyers: 37.
[3] *A Life in Letters:* 17.
[4] Meyers: 37.
[5] Nancy Milford, *Zelda* (New York, 1970): 8.
[6] Ibid: 15.
[7] Ibid: 22.
[8] *A Life in Letters:* 22.
[9] *This Side of Paradise:* 140.
[10] Ibid: 173.
[11] Ibid: 260.
[12] Quoted in Patrick O'Donnell, "Introduction" in *This Side of Paradise:* xii.
[13] Quoted in Meyers: 51.

CHAPTER 4

[1] *The Crack-Up:* 89.
[2] Quoted in Le Vot: 74.
[3] *A Life in Letters:* 37.
[4] Quoted in O'Donnell: xviii-xix.
[5] *The Crack-Up:* 87.
[6] *A Life in Letters:* 44.
[7] LeVot: 111.
[8] *The Beautiful and Damned:* 449.
[9] Ibid: 58.
[10] Ibid: 304.
[11] Ibid: 449.
[12] Quoted in Meyers: 89.

[13] Ibid: 90.
[14] Zelda Fitzgerald, *The Collected Writings of Zelda Fitzgerald*, ed. Mathew J. Bruccoli (Tuscaloosa, 1991): 387.
[15] Ibid: 388.

CHAPTER 5

[1] *The Great Gatsby:* 182.
[2] Le Vot: 119.
[3] *A Life in Letters:* 67.
[4] Meyers: 113.
[5] *A Life in Letters:* 79.
[6] Ibid: 95–6.
[7] Ibid: 85.
[8] Ibid: 80.
[9] *The Great Gatsby:* 41.
[10] Ibid: 97.
[11] Ibid: 120.
[12] Ibid: 154.
[13] Ibid: 160.
[14] Quoted in Meyers: 130.
[15] Ibid: 129.
[16] Ibid: 130.

CHAPTER 6

[1] F. Scott Fitzgerald, *The Short Stories of F. Scott Fitzgerald*, ed. Matthew J. Bruccoli (New York, 1989): 616.
[2] *A Life in Letters:* 82.
[3] Ernest Hemingway, *A Moveable Feast* (New York, 1964): 149.
[4] Le Vot: 191.
[5] Quoted in Meyers: 155.
[6] *A Life in Letters:* 130.
[7] Mizener: 79.
[8] Meyers: 166–7.
[9] *A Life in Letters:* 148.
[10] Mellow: 279.
[11] Meyers: 174.
[12] Mellow: 308.
[13] Meyers: 178.
[14] *A Life in Letters:* 181.

CHAPTER 7

[1] F. Scott Fitzgerald, *Tender Is the Night* (New York, 1986): 168.
[2] Milford: 158.
[3] Ibid: 159–60.
[4] *A Life in Letters:* 197.
[5] Ibid: 189.
[6] Zelda Fitzgerald: 450.
[7] Quoted in LeVot: 257.
[8] Zelda Fitzgerald: 460.
[9] *A Life in Letters:* 209.
[10] Zelda Fitzgerald: 105,13.
[11] *Tender Is the Night:* 15.
[12] Ibid: 190–91.
[13] Ibid: 298.

CHAPTER 8

[1] F. Scott Fitzgerald, *The Last Tycoon* (New York, 1969): 148.
[2] Charles Scribner II, "Introduction" in *Tender Is the Night:* xiii.
[3] Ibid: xii.
[4] Le Vot: 246.
[5] Ibid: 277.
[6] *A Life in Letters:* 291.
[7] *The Crack-Up:* 69.
[8] Ibid: 79.
[9] Ibid: 83.
[10] Zelda Fitzgerald: 479.
[11] *A Life in Letters:* 306.
[12] Ibid: 314.
[13] Meyers: 289; Le Vot: 318–19.
[14] Ibid: 332.
[15] *The Last Tycoon:* 29.
[16] *A Life in Letters:* 474.
[17] Ibid: 475.
[18] Le Vot: 352.
[19] Meyers: 336.

EPILOGUE

[1] *A Life in Letters:* 131.
[2] Meyers: 338.

INDEX

9/23/02 ✓